Acting Edition

Romeo and Julius [Caesar]

by William Shakespeare
& Jeff Goode

Copyright © 2007, 2008 by Jeff Goode
All Rights Reserved

ROMEO AND JULIUS [CAESAR] is fully protected under the copyright laws of the United States of America, the British Commonwealth, including Canada, and all member countries of the Berne Convention for the Protection of Literary and Artistic Works, the Universal Copyright Convention, and/or the World Trade Organization conforming to the Agreement on Trade Related Aspects of Intellectual Property Rights. All rights, including professional and amateur stage productions, recitation, lecturing, public reading, motion picture, radio broadcasting, television, online/digital production, and the rights of translation into foreign languages are strictly reserved.

ISBN 978-0-87440-280-3

www.concordtheatricals.com
www.concordtheatricals.co.uk

FOR PRODUCTION INQUIRIES

UNITED STATES AND CANADA
info@concordtheatricals.com
1-866-979-0447

UNITED KINGDOM AND EUROPE
licensing@concordtheatricals.co.uk
020-7054-7298

Each title is subject to availability from Concord Theatricals Corp., depending upon country of performance. Please be aware that *ROMEO AND JULIUS [CAESAR]* may not be licensed by Concord Theatricals Corp. in your territory. Professional and amateur producers should contact the nearest Concord Theatricals Corp. office or licensing partner to verify availability.

CAUTION: Professional and amateur producers are hereby warned that *ROMEO AND JULIUS [CAESAR]* is subject to a licensing fee. The purchase, renting, lending or use of this book does not constitute a license to perform this title(s), which license must be obtained from Concord Theatricals Corp. prior to any performance. Performance of this title(s) without a license is a violation of federal law and may subject the producer and/or presenter of such performances to civil penalties. Both amateurs and professionals considering a production are strongly advised to apply to the appropriate agent before starting rehearsals, advertising, or booking a theatre. A licensing fee must be paid whether the title(s) is presented for charity or gain and whether or not admission is charged. Professional/Stock licensing fees are quoted upon application to Concord Theatricals Corp.

This work is published by Samuel French, an imprint of Concord Theatricals Corp.

No one shall make any changes in this title(s) for the purpose of production. No part of this book may be reproduced, stored in a retrieval system, scanned, uploaded, or transmitted in any form, by any means, now known or yet to be invented, including mechanical, electronic, digital, photocopying, recording, videotaping, or otherwise, without the prior written permission of the publisher. No one shall share this title(s), or any part of this title(s), through any social media or file hosting websites.

For all inquiries regarding motion picture, television, online/digital and other media rights, please contact Concord Theatricals Corp.

MUSIC AND THIRD-PARTY MATERIALS USE NOTE

Licensees are solely responsible for obtaining formal written permission from copyright owners to use copyrighted music and/or other copyrighted third-party materials (e.g., artworks, logos) in the performance of this play and are strongly cautioned to do so. If no such permission is obtained by the licensee, then the licensee must use only original music and materials that the licensee owns and controls. Licensees are solely responsible and liable for clearances of all third-party copyrighted materials, including without limitation music, and shall indemnify the copyright owners of the play(s) and their licensing agent, Concord Theatricals Corp., against any costs, expenses, losses and liabilities arising from the use of such copyrighted third-party materials by licensees. For music, please contact the appropriate music licensing authority in your territory for the rights to any incidental music.

IMPORTANT BILLING AND CREDIT REQUIREMENTS

If you have obtained performance rights to this title, please refer to your licensing agreement for important billing and credit requirements.

my eternal thanks to
SEAN MARLOW
for the inspiration and encouragement.

PREFACE

They say that "familiarity breeds contempt" and there is no playwright, living or dead, whose work is more familiar to audiences the world over, than William Shakespeare. Four hundred years of almost continuous production, adaptation and recitation have ensured that even the completely uninitiated have a working knowledge of the Bard that can render some of his finest works formulaic.

What grade-schooler doesn't know that the love affair in *Romeo and Juliet* turns out badly? Or that the famous speech in *Hamlet* goes: "To be, or not to be, yadda yadda yadda..."? And in a medium where suspense is everything—where dramatic twists and comic turns both depend upon the element of surprise—having such a well-versed fan-base can be problematic. Ironically, the most gifted dramatist in history is often hard-pressed to impress our jaded modern audience, simply because it is impossible to remove their foreknowledge of the story and allow them to experience the plays in the unadulterated context in which Shakespeare's contemporaries saw them for the very first time.

The Shakespeare Fusion Series was developed as a means to a fresh perspective on these classic texts. Each play in the series intertwines two of the extant works to create an original script with authentically Shakespearean language, verse and characters, in new and unexpected stories and situations whose outcome may still be in doubt.

The plays in this series are designed to be read, performed and enjoyed just as you would the traditional works of Shakespeare. Actors familiar with the canon will find that great lengths have been taken to preserve the integrity and intention of the original verse, rhyme and imagery. Conventions of Elizabethan stagecraft, dramaturgical analysis and scansion apply to the new plays as to the originals. Only the action is up in the air.

The series also seeks to address a handful of challenges common to present day production companies, such as cast size and balance of male and female roles.

It is hoped that these plays might offer both performers and audiences new insight into the genius and mastery of Shakespeare, freed of a few centuries' preconception, and perhaps with a few surprises still intact.

Romeo & Julius [Caesar] was performed March 8th, 2004, as part of the Washington Shakespeare Company's "Arlington Dramatist Project". The production was directed by Scott Bradley with the following company:

Ian Armstrong, Fiona Blackshaw, Melissa Flaim,
Chris Galindo, Christopher Henley, Annie Houston,
Scott Kerns, Daniel Ladmirault, Anne Nottage,
Tyee Tilghman & Steve Wilhite

ROMEO'S ROMA

The election of the charismatic and openly-gay Julius Caesar to the office once held by moralistic Pompey heralds an era of unprecedented tolerance in Republican Rome. However, Caesar's rise to power, while popular with the Commoners, has engendered animosity among conservative factions in the Senate—led by family man Caius Cassius—who believe that Caesar intends to flout their values with an agenda of aggressive social reforms, and even moderates such as Caesar's companion Marcus Brutus are concerned that he may have gone too far.

With the approach of Lupercal—the Roman "Pride" Festival, now elevated to a national holiday—outraged reactionaries have taken to the streets to protest the burgeoning decadence, making Rome, once again, a dangerous place for a young man to explore his sexuality.

DRAMATIS PERSONAE

FLAVIUS CIMBER, *a Roman tribune*
METELLUS CIMBER, *his brother*
SAMPSON, *a commoner*
GREGORY, *his lover*
BENVOLIO, *cousin to Gregory*
JULIUS CAESAR, *a flamboyant Roman politician*
MARCUS BRUTUS
CINNA } *conspirators against Julius Caesar*
CAIUS CASSIUS
NURSE, *bondwoman to Cassius*
ROMEO, *son to Cassius*
PORTIA, *wife to Brutus*
LUCIUS, *attendant to Brutus*
ROSALINE, *a Soothsayer*
CINNA, *a poet*

Citizens, Attendants, Revelers, Soldiers, etc.

Prologue

Two causes, both of like indignity,
In Caesar's Roma, where we lay our scene,
From grudging tolerance breed new mutiny,
When civil pride rates other pride unclean.
From forth the fatal factions of these foes
Two star-cross'd lovers find each other out;
Whose misadventured piteous overthrows
Do with their courtship cast all Rome in doubt.
The fearful passage of their hate-mark'd love,
And the insurgence of much righteous rage,
Which, but great Caesar's end, nought could remove,
Is now the two hours' traffic of our stage;
The which if you with patient ears attend,
What here shall miss, our toil shall strive to mend.

ACT I

SCENE 1
Rome. A street. Before a statue of Pompey.

(*Enter certain flamboyant Commoners to dance the Lupercal. They bear garlands of lavender and ladies' scarfs to deck great Pompey's statue withal. Last, they bring in a lady's wig to crown it.*)

(*Enter two surly Romans,* **FLAVIUS** *and* **METELLUS CIMBER**, *armed with swords and bucklers, to fright the Commoners.*)

FLAVIUS CIMBER. Hence! home, you idle creatures get you home!

METELLUS CIMBER. Go, go, good countrymen, run to your houses!

(*They chase them away with their swords.*)

FLAVIUS CIMBER. Metellus, see; their basest mettle moved,
They vanish tongue-tied in their guiltiness.
Go you down that way towards the Capitol;
This way will I disrobe the images,
If you do find them deck'd with ceremonies.

METELLUS CIMBER. May we do so?
You know it is the feast of Lupercal.

FLAVIUS CIMBER. It is no matter; let no images
Be hung with Caesar's bawdies. I'll about,
And drive away the vulgar from the streets:
So do you too, where you perceive them thick.
These gaudy feathers pluck'd from Caesar's wing
Will make him fly an ordinary pitch,
Who else would soar above the view of men
And keep us all in shameful servitude.

(*They remove garlands from the statue and trample them on the ground.*)

(*Enter another pair of Commoners,* **GREGORY** *and* **SAMPSON**, *bearing more flowers.*)

GREGORY. (*Aside to* **SAMPSON**) Draw thy tool! here stands two of the house of Cassius.

(*Drawing his awl.*)

SAMPSON. Let us take the law of our sides; let them begin.

GREGORY. I will frown as I pass by, and let them take it as they list.

SAMPSON. Nay, as they dare.

(**FLAVIUS** *and* **METELLUS CIMBER** *notice them and advance upon* **GREGORY** *and* **SAMPSON**.)

FLAVIUS CIMBER. Is this a holiday? what! know you not,
   Being mechanical, you ought not walk
   Upon a labouring day without the sign
   Of your profession? Speak, what trade art thou?
SAMPSON. Why, sir, a carpenter.
METELLUS CIMBER. Where is thy leather apron and thy rule?
   What dost thou with thy best apparel on?
   You, sir, what trade are you?
SAMPSON. (*Aside to* **GREGORY**) Quarrel, I will back thee.
GREGORY. How! turn thy back and run?
SAMPSON. Fear me not.
GREGORY. No, marry; I fear thee!
METELLUS CIMBER. What trade art thou? answer me directly.
GREGORY. A trade, sir, that, I hope, I may use with a safe conscience; which is, indeed, sir, a mender of bad soles.
FLAVIUS CIMBER. What trade, thou knave? thou naughty knave, what trade?
GREGORY. Nay, I beseech you, sir, be not out with me.
SAMPSON. Yet, if you be *out*, sir, he can mend you.
FLAVIUS CIMBER. What meanest thou by that? mend me, thou saucy fellow!
GREGORY. Why, sir, cobble you.
METELLUS CIMBER. Thou art a cobbler, art thou?
GREGORY. I am, indeed, sir, a surgeon to old shoes; when they are in great danger, I recover them.
METELLUS CIMBER. But wherefore art not in thy shop today?
   Why dost thou lead this man about the streets?
GREGORY. Truly, sir, to wear out his shoes, to get myself into more work. But, indeed, sir, we make holiday, to see Caesar and to rejoice in his triumph.

   (*A Crowd begins to gather.*)

FLAVIUS CIMBER. Wherefore rejoice? What conquest brings he home?
What tributaries follow him to Rome,
To grace in captive bonds his chariot-wheels?
You blocks, you stones, you worse than senseless things!
O you hard hearts, you cruel men of Rome,
Knew you not Pompey? There's a man of honour!
And such a man that many a time and oft
Have you climb'd up to walls and battlements,
To towers and windows, yea, and there have sat
The livelong day, with patient expectation,
To see great Pompey pass the streets of Rome:
And when you saw his chariot but appear,
Have you not made an universal shout,
That Tiber trembled underneath her banks,
To hear the replication of your sounds
Made in her concave shores?
And do you now put on your best attire?
And do you now cull out a holiday?
And do you now strew flowers in his way
That is unfit to bow at Pompey's feet?
Be gone! Run to your houses, fall upon your knees,
Pray to the gods to intermit the plague
That needs must light on this insanctity.

SAMPSON. (*Aside to* **GREGORY**) I will bite my thumb at them; which is a disgrace to them, if they bear it.

FLAVIUS CIMBER. Do you bite your thumb at us, sir?

SAMPSON. I do bite my thumb, sir.

METELLUS CIMBER. Do you bite your thumb at us, sir?

SAMPSON. (*Aside to* **GREGORY**) Is the law of our side, if I say 'Ay'?

GREGORY. No.

SAMPSON. No, sir, I do not bite my thumb at you, sir, but I bite my thumb, sir.

GREGORY. Do you quarrel, sir?

FLAVIUS CIMBER. Quarrel sir! no, sir.

SAMPSON. If you do, sir, I am for you: I am as good a man as you.

METELLUS CIMBER. No better?

SAMPSON. Well, sir.

GREGORY. Say 'better:' here comes one of my kinsmen.

SAMPSON. Yes, better, sir.

METELLUS CIMBER. You lie.

FLAVIUS CIMBER. Draw, if you be men.

(*They fight; The Commoners are outmatched.*)

(*Enter* **GREGORY***'s kinswoman,* **BENVOLIO**.)

BENVOLIO. Part, fools! Put up your swords; you know not what you do.

(*Beats down their swords*)

FLAVIUS CIMBER. What, art thou drawn to help these heartless hinds?

Turn thee, Benvolio, look upon thy death.

BENVOLIO. I do but keep the peace: put up thy sword,
Or manage it to part these men with me.

FLAVIUS CIMBER. What, drawn, and talk of peace! I hate the word,
As I hate hell, all heretics, and thee:
Have at thee, coward!

(*They fight.*)

(*Enter, several of both factions, who join the fray.*)

BENVOLIO. Gentlemen, for shame, forbear this outrage!

(*Enter Citizens, with clubs to break up the fight.*)

FIRST CITIZEN. Clubs, bills, and partisans! strike! beat them down!

BENVOLIO. Good gentle Flavius, put thy rapier up.

FLAVIUS CIMBER. I will not till my rapier put thee down!

(**FLAVIUS** *stabs* **BENVOLIO**.)

METELLUS CIMBER. Hold Flavius!

GREGORY. Good Benvolio!

BENVOLIO. I am hurt.

A plague o' both your causes! I am sped.

SAMPSON. What, art thou hurt?

BENVOLIO. Ay, ay, a scratch, a scratch; marry, 'tis enough.

GREGORY. Courage, coz; the hurt cannot be much.

BENVOLIO. No, 'tis not so deep as a well, nor so wide as a church-door; but 'tis enough, 'twill serve: ask for me to-morrow, and you shall find me a grave woman. Why the devil came I between you?

GREGORY. You thought all for the best.

BENVOLIO. Help me into some house, or I shall faint.

A plague o' both your causes!

They have made worms' meat of me.

(*Dies*)

METELLUS CIMBER. Flavius, away, be gone!

The citizens are up, Benvolio slain.

Stand not amazed: The law expressly hath

Forbid this bandying in the Roman streets.

Go, Flavius, brother, flee: Caesar will doom thee death,

If thou art taken: hence, be gone, away!

FLAVIUS CIMBER. I will not budge for no man's pleasure, I.

(*Enter Citizens of the Guard.*)

FIRST CITIZEN. Which way ran he that kill'd Benvolio?

Flavius, that murderer, which way ran he?

FLAVIUS CIMBER. Here stands that Flavius.

FIRST CITIZEN. Come, sir, go with me;

I charge thee in great Caesar's name, obey.

(*Enter* **CAESAR** *bedecked with scarfs and garlands of lavender – like Pompey's statue – and with him,* **BRUTUS**, **PORTIA**, *Attendants and others.*)

BRUTUS. Where are the vile beginners of this fray?

GREGORY. O noble sir, I can discover all
  The unlucky manage of this fatal brawl:
  There is the man, that murderer Flavius,
  That slew my cousin, brave Benvolio.
METELLUS CIMBER. He is a kinsman to Benvolio;
  Affection makes him false; he speaks not true.
BRUTUS. Metellus, who began this bloody fray?

(**FLAVIUS** *interjects, accusing* **SAMPSON** *and* **GREGORY**.)

FLAVIUS CIMBER. Here were two spatting ere we did approach:
  I drew to part them: in the instant came
  The brash Benvolio, with her sword prepared,
  Which, as she breathed defiance to my ears,
  She swung about her head and cut the winds,
  Who nothing hurt withal hiss'd her in scorn:
  While we were interchanging thrusts and blows,
  Came more and more and fought on part and part,
  Till Caesar came, who parted either part.

(**GREGORY** *lunges at* **FLAVIUS**. **SAMPSON** *holds him back.*)

GREGORY. Thou liest, villain—Hold me not, let me go.
FLAVIUS CIMBER. Wilt thou provoke me? then have at thee, boy!

(**FLAVIUS** *draws to fight again.*)

CAESAR. Rebellious subjects, enemies to peace,
  That quench the fire of your pernicious rage
  With purple fountains issuing from your veins,
  On pain of torture, from those bloody hands
  Throw your mistemper'd weapons to the ground,
  And hear the sentence of your movèd Caesar.
  Three civil brawls born of intolerance
  Have thrice disturbed the quiet of our streets.
  If ever you disturb our streets again,
  Your lives shall pay the forfeit of the peace.

(*Commoners grumble at the injustice.*)

And for Flavius,
Immediately we do exile him hence:

(**FLAVIUS** *and* **METELLUS** *also grumble.*)

I will be deaf to pleading and excuses;
Nor tears nor prayers shall purchase out abuses:
Therefore use none: let Flavius hence in haste,
Else, when he's ta'en, that hour is his last.

(*Enter* **CASSIUS** *and the* **NURSE**, *who join the growing Crowd.*)

For this time, all the rest depart away:
Come, Brutus, you shall go along with me:
Once more, on pain of death, all men depart.
Bear hence this body and attend our will:
Mercy but murders, pardoning those that kill.

(**CAESAR** *takes* **BRUTUS** *by the hand and departs; the crowd follows after him.*)

NURSE. (*to a Passerby*) Gentlemen, can any of you tell me where I may find young Romeo?

(*The Commoners ignore her, or bite their thumb at her, as they leave.*)

(*Exeunt all but* **CASSIUS**, *the* **NURSE**, *and* **METELLUS CIMBER**.)

CASSIUS. What set this controversy now abroach?
Speak, cousin, were you by when it began?

METELLUS CIMBER. My brother Flavius, but for pulling scarfs
Off Caesar's images, is put to exile.

CASSIUS. O outrage! Banishment? Is't possible?
Iniquity plucks justice by the nose.
It fits, when such a villain is enthroned:
I cannot tell what you and other men
Think of this life; but, for my single self,

I had as lief not be as live to be
In awe of such a thing as Caesar is.
I was born free as Caesar; and this man
Is now become a god, and Cassius is
A wretched creature and must bend his body,
If Caesar carelessly but nod on him.
Ye gods, it doth amaze me
A man of such a feeble virtue should
So get the start of the majestic world
And bear the palm alone.

NURSE. O, where is Romeo? saw you him to-day?
Right glad I am he was not at this fray.

METELLUS CIMBER. Madam, beneath the grove of sycamore
That westward rooteth from the city's side,
So early walking did I see your charge:
Towards him I made, but he was ware of me
And stole into the covert of the wood:
I, measuring his affections by my own,
That most are busied when they're most alone,
Pursued my humour not pursuing his,
And gladly shunn'd who gladly fled from me.

CASSIUS. Many a morning hath he there been seen,
With tears augmenting the fresh morning dew.
Adding to clouds more clouds with his deep sighs.

NURSE. But all so soon as the all-cheering sun
Should in the furthest east begin to draw
The shady curtains from Aurora's bed,
Away from the light steals home young Romeò,
And private in his chamber pens himself,
Shuts up his windows, locks fair daylight out
And makes himself an artificial night.

CASSIUS. Black and portentous must this humour prove,
Unless good counsel may the cause remove.

METELLUS CIMBER. My noble Cassius, do you know the cause?

NURSE. Could we but learn from whence his sorrows grow.
We would as willingly give cure as know.

(*Enter* **ROMEO**.)

METELLUS CIMBER. See, where he comes: so please you, step aside;
I'll know his grievance, or be much denied.

CASSIUS. I would thou wert so happy by thy stay,
To hear true shrift. God speed you; let's away.

(*Exit* **CASSIUS** *and* **NURSE**.)

METELLUS CIMBER. Good-morrow, Romeo.

ROMEO. Is the day so young?

METELLUS CIMBER. But new struck nine.

ROMEO. Ay me! sad hours seem long.
Was that my father that went hence so fast?

METELLUS CIMBER. It was. What sadness lengthens Romeo's hours?

ROMEO. Not having that, which, having, makes them short.

METELLUS CIMBER. In love?

ROMEO. Out.

METELLUS CIMBER. Of love?

ROMEO. Out of her favour, where I am in love.

METELLUS CIMBER. Alas, that love, so gentle in his view,
Should be so tyrannous and rough in proof!

ROMEO. Alas, that love, whose view is muffled still,
Should, without eyes, see pathways to his will!
Where shall we dine? O me! What fray was here?
Yet tell me not, for I have heard it all.
Here's much to do with hate, but more with love.
Why, then, O brawling love! O loving hate!
O any thing, of nothing first create!
O heavy lightness! serious vanity!

Still-waking sleep, that is not what it is!
This love feel I, that feel no love in this.
Dost thou not laugh?

METELLUS CIMBER. No, coz, I rather weep.

ROMEO. Good heart, at what?

METELLUS CIMBER. At thy good heart's oppression.

ROMEO. Why, such is love's transgression.
Love is a smoke raised with the fume of sighs;
Being purged, a fire sparkling in lovers' eyes;
Being vex'd a sea nourish'd with lovers' tears:
What is it else? a madness most discreet,
A choking gall and a preserving sweet.
Cousin, farewell.

METELLUS CIMBER. Soft! I will go along;
An if you leave me so, you do me wrong.

ROMEO. Tut, I have lost myself; I am not here;
This is not Romeo, he's some other where.

METELLUS CIMBER. Tell me in sadness, who is that you love.

ROMEO. What, shall I groan and tell thee?

METELLUS CIMBER. Groan! why, no.
But sadly tell me who.

ROMEO. In sadness, cousin, I do love a woman.

METELLUS CIMBER. I aim'd so near, when I supposed you loved.

ROMEO. A right good mark-man! And she's fair I love.

METELLUS CIMBER. A right fair mark, fair coz, is soonest hit.

ROMEO. Well, in that hit you miss: she'll not be hit
With Cupid's arrow; she hath Dian's wit;
And, in strong proof of chastity well arm'd,
From love's weak childish bow she lives unharm'd.
She will not stay the siege of loving terms,
Nor bide the encounter of assailing eyes,

Nor ope her lap to saint-seducing gold:
O, she is rich in beauty, only poor,
That when she dies with beauty dies her store.

METELLUS CIMBER. Then she hath sworn that she will still live chaste?

ROMEO. She hath, and in that sparing makes huge waste,
For beauty starved with her severity
Cuts beauty off from all posterity.
She hath forsworn to love, and in that vow
Do I live dead that live to tell it now.

METELLUS CIMBER. Why, Romeo, art thou mad?

ROMEO. Not mad, but bound more than a mad-man is;
Shut up in prison, kept without my food,
Whipp'd and tormented and—See where she comes.

(*Enter* **ROSALINE** *the* **SOOTHSAYER**.)

METELLUS CIMBER. Is this thy love? the soothsayer Rosaline?

ROMEO. God-den, fair lady.

SOOTHSAYER. God gi' god-den, good fellow.

(*The* **SOOTHSAYER** *tries to pass, but* **ROMEO** *blocks her path.*)

ROMEO. Come hither, mistress: which way hast thou been?

SOOTHSAYER. At mine own house, good fellow.
What is't o'clock?

ROMEO. About the ninth hour, lady.

SOOTHSAYER. Is Caesar yet gone to the Lupercal?
I go to take my stand,
To see him pass on to the Capitol.

ROMEO. Jesu, what haste? can you not stay awhile?
Tarry here, I'll mark his passage with thee.

SOOTHSAYER. Here the street is narrow:
The throng that follows Caesar at the heels,
Of senators, of praetors, common suitors,
Will crowd a feeble maid almost to death:

I'll get me to a place more void, and there
Speak to great Caesar as he comes along.

ROMEO. Thou hast some suit to Caesar, hast thou not?

SOOTHSAYER. That I have, fellow: if it will please Caesar. To be so good to Caesar as to hear me,
I shall beseech him to befriend himself.

ROMEO. Why, know'st thou any harm's intended towards him?

SOOTHSAYER. None that I know will be, much that I fear may chance.
Good morrow to you.

(**SOOTHSAYER** *exits.*)

ROMEO. She is too fair, too wise, wisely too fair,
To merit bliss by making me despair.

METELLUS CIMBER. Be ruled by me, forget to think of her.

ROMEO. O, teach me how I should forget to think.

METELLUS CIMBER. By giving liberty unto thine eyes;
Examine other beauties.

ROMEO. 'Tis the way
To call hers exquisite, in question more:
Show me a mistress that is passing fair,
What doth her beauty serve, but as a note
Where I may read who pass'd that passing fair?

METELLUS CIMBER. To this same Caesar's feast of Lupercal
Wends the fair Rosaline whom thou so lovest,
With all the admirèd beauties of the city:
Go thither; and, with unattainted eye,
Compare her face with some that I shall show,
And I will make thee think thy swan a crow.

ROMEO. I'll go along, no such sight to be shown,
But to rejoice in splendor of mine own.

(*Exeunt*)

SCENE 2
Before Caesar's house.

(*Flourish.* **CAESAR** *makes his grand entrance in a lavish lavender ball gown and wigged. He greets the Guests and Maskers, among them the* **SOOTHSAYER**; **BRUTUS**, **PORTIA**, **CINNA**, **CASSIUS**, *and* **NURSE**.)

CAESAR. This night I hold an old accustomed feast,
Whereto I have invited many a guest,
Such as I love; and you among the store.

(*Guests chuckle at his jest.*)

Each one, most welcome, makes my number more.
At my poor house look to behold this night
Earth-treading stars that make dark heaven light.
Such comfort as do lusty young men feel
When well-appareled April on the heel
Of limping winter treads, even such delight
Shall you inherit at my house this night.
Come go with me to feast the Lupercal
If pride be sin, we'll damnèd be withal.
For lovers, friends, or both, to you I say
My house and welcome on your pleasures stay!

SOOTHSAYER. Caesar!

CAESAR. Ha! who calls?

CINNA. Bid every noise be still: peace yet again!

CAESAR. Who is it in the press that calls on me?
I hear a tongue, shriller than all the music,
Cry 'Caesar!' Speak; Caesar is turn'd to hear.

SOOTHSAYER. Beware the ides of March.

CAESAR. What woman's that?

BRUTUS. A soothsayer bids you beware the ides of March.

CAESAR. Set her before me; let me see her face.

BRUTUS. You, there, come from the throng; look upon Caesar.

CAESAR. What say'st thou to me now? speak once again.
SOOTHSAYER. Beware the ides of March.
CAESAR. She is a dreamer; let us leave her: dance!

(*Music plays, and they dance. Women dance with women. Men dance with other men.*)

(*Enter* **ROMEO** *and* **METELLUS CIMBER**.)

METELLUS CIMBER. Come, gentle Romeo, we must have you dance.
ROMEO. Not I, believe me. You have dancing shoes
With nimble soles; I have a soul of lead
So stakes me to the ground I cannot move.

MERCUTIO
You are a lover. Borrow Cupid's Wings
And soar with them above a common bound.

ROMEO. I am too sore enpiercèd with his shaft
To soar with his light feathers; and so bound
I cannot bound a pitch above dull woe.
Under love's heavy burden do I sink.

(**CAESAR** *ushers the Revelers into the house.*)

CAESAR. Welcome, gentlemen! ladies that have their toes
Unplagued with corns will have a bout with you.
Ah ha, my mistresses! which of you all
Will now deny to dance? she that makes dainty,
She, I'll swear, hath corns; Come, musicians, play.
A hall, a hall! give room! and foot it, girls.

(*More music, and dancing;* **CAESAR** *cuts in on* **BRUTUS** *and* **PORTIA** *and dances away with her husband.*)

ROMEO. O, she doth teach the torches to burn bright!
It seems she hangs upon the cheek of night
Like a rich jewel in an Ethiope's ear;
Beauty too rich for use, for earth too dear!
(*To* **METELLUS CIMBER**) What lady is that, which doth enrich the hand
Of yonder knight?

(**METELLUS** *laughs.*)

METELLUS CIMBER. Why, know you not, sir? That is Julius Caesar.

(*He withdraws, laughing still.*)

ROMEO. So shows a snowy dove trooping with crows,
As yonder Caesar o'er his fellows shows.
Did my heart love till now? forswear it, sight!
For I ne'er saw true beauty till this night.
The measure done, I'll watch his place of stand,
And, touching his, make blessèd my rude hand.

(**ROMEO** *follows the revelers into the house. Exeunt all but* **CASSIUS**, **METELLUS** *and* **NURSE**.)

CASSIUS. How now, Metellus! What says Romeò?
What news, my nephew? Hast thou spoke with him?

METELLUS CIMBER. This is the matter—

CASSIUS. Nurse, give leave awhile,
We must talk in secret. Nurse, come back again;
I have remembered me, thou's hear our counsel.

METELLUS CIMBER. A pale hard-hearted wench, that Rosaline. Torments him so, that he will sure run mad.

CASSIUS. The Soothsayer Rosaline?

NURSE. O, she is fair!
And a good lady, and a wise and virtuous.

METELLUS CIMBER. Tut, he saw her fair, none else being by,
Herself poised with herself in either eye:
But in that crystal scales let there be weigh'd
His ladylove against some other maid
That I will show him shining at this feast,
And she shall scant show well that now shows best.

(*The* **NURSE** *falls to sobbing.*)

CASSIUS. All this is comfort; wherefore weepest thou?

NURSE. He was the prettiest babe that e'er I nursed.

An I might live to see him married once
I have my wish.
'Tis since the earthquake now eleven years;
And he was weaned (I never shall forget it),
Of all the days of the year, upon that day,
For I had then laid wormwood to my dug,
Sitting in the sun under the dove-house wall.
My Lord and I were then at Mantua.
Nay, I do bear a brain. But, as I said,
When it did taste the wormwood on the nipple
Of my dug and felt it bitter, pretty fool,
To see it tetchy and fall out with the dug!
'Shake,' quoth the dove-house! 'Twas no need, I trow,
To bid me trudge.
And since that time it is eleven years,
For then he could stand high-lone; nay, by th'rood,
He could have run and waddled all about;
For even the day before, he broke his brow,
And then my husband (God be with his soul!
A' was a merry man) took up the child.
'Yea,' quoth he, 'dost thou fall upon thy face?
Thou wilt fall backward when thou has more wit;
Wilt thou not, boy?' and, by my holidam,
The pretty wretch left crying and said 'Ay.'
To see now how a jest shall come about!
I warrant, an I should live a thousand years,
I never should forget it. 'Wilt thou not, boy?' quoth he,
And, pretty fool, it stinted and said 'Ay.'

CASSIUS. And stint thou too, I pray thee, nurse, say I.

NURSE. Peace, I have done.

CASSIUS. For all this same, I'll seek her at this feast:
    And will acquaint her here of my son's love
    That reason may her chaste affections move.

METELLUS. And you mean well to hasten such a match;
    But 'tis no wit to do so.

CASSIUS. Why, is that?

Younger than they are happy couples made.

METELLUS. And too soon marred are those so early made.

(*They withdraw.*)

(*Re-enter* **PORTIA**, *leaving the party in a huff.* **BRUTUS** *tries to stay her.*)

BRUTUS. Why, how now, Portia! wherefore storm you so?

PORTIA. Griefs of mine own lie heavy in my breast,
    Which thou wilt propagate, to have it prest
    With more of thine: this love that thou hast shown
    Doth add more grief to too much of mine own.

BRUTUS. Poor soul, thy face is much abused with tears.

PORTIA. The tears have got small victory by that;
    For it was bad enough before their spite.

BRUTUS. 'Tis Julius grieves thee?

PORTIA. 'Tis he, that lecherous Caesar.

BRUTUS. Content thee, gentle wife, let him alone;
    I would not for the wealth of all the town
    Here in his house do him disparagement:
    Therefore be patient, take no note of him:
    It is my will, the which if thou respect,
    Show a fair presence and put off these frowns,
    And ill-beseeming semblance for a feast.

PORTIA. I'll not endure him.

BRUTUS. He shall be endured:
    Am I the husband here, or you? go to.
    You'll not endure him! God shall mend my soul!
    You'll make a mutiny among the guests!
    You will set cock-a-hoop! you'll be the man!

PORTIA. Why, husband, 'tis a shame.

BRUTUS. Go to, go to;
    You must contrary me! Hence, home to bed!

(**PORTIA** *exits;* **BRUTUS** *broods.* **CASSIUS** *comes forward.*)

CASSIUS. Brutus, I do observe you now of late:

I have not from your eyes that gentleness
And show of love as I was wont to have:
You bear too stubborn and too strange a hand
Over your friend that loves you.

BRUTUS. Cassius,
Be not deceived: if I have veil'd my look,
I turn the trouble of my countenance
Merely upon myself. Vexèd I am
Of late with passions of some difference,
Conceptions only proper to myself,
Which give some soil perhaps to my behaviors;
But let not therefore my good friends be grieved
(Among which number, Cassius, be you one)
Nor construe any further my neglect,
Than that poor Brutus, with himself at war,
Forgets the shows of love to other men.

CASSIUS. Then, Brutus, I have much mistook your passion;
By means whereof this breast of mine hath buried
Thoughts of great value, worthy cogitations.
Tell me, good Brutus, can you see your face?

BRUTUS. No, Cassius; for the eye sees not itself,
But by reflection, by some other things.

CASSIUS. 'Tis just:
And it is very much lamented, Brutus,
That you have no such mirrors as will turn
Your hidden worthiness into your eye,
That you might see your shadow. I have heard,
Where many of the best respect in Rome,
Except immortal Caesar, speaking of Brutus. And groaning underneath this age's yoke,
Have wish'd that noble Brutus had his eyes.

BRUTUS. Into what dangers would you lead me, Cassius,
That you would have me seek into myself
For that which is not in me?

CASSIUS. Therefore, good Brutus, be prepared to hear:
  And since you know you cannot see yourself
  So well as by reflection, I, your glass,
  Will modestly discover to yourself
  That of yourself which you yet know not of
  And be not jealous on me, gentle Brutus:
  Were I a common laugher, or did use
  To stale with ordinary oaths my love
  To every new protester; if you know
  That I do fawn on men and hug them hard
  And after scandal them, or if you know
  That I profess myself in banqueting
  To all the rout, then hold me dangerous.

  (*Flourish, and shout.*)

BRUTUS. What means this shouting? I do fear, the people
  Choose Caesar for their king.

CASSIUS. Ay, do you fear it?
  Then must I think you would not have it so.

BRUTUS. I would not, Cassius; yet I love him well.
  What is it that you would impart to me?
  If it be aught toward the general good,
  Set honour in one eye and death i' the other,
  And I will look on both indifferently,
  For let the gods so speed me as I love
  The name of honour more than I fear death.

  (*Shout. Flourish.*)

  Another general shout!
  I do believe that these applauses are
  For some new honours that are heap'd on Caesar.

CASSIUS. Why, man, he doth bestride the narrow world
  Like a Colossus, and we petty men
  Walk under his huge legs and peep about
  To find ourselves dishonourable graves.
  Men at some time are masters of their fates:
  The fault, dear Brutus, is not in our stars,

But in ourselves, that we are underlings.
Now, in the names of all the gods at once,
Upon what meat doth this our Caesar feed,
That he is grown so great? Age, thou art shamed!
Rome, thou hast lost the breed of noble bloods!
O, you and I have heard our fathers say,
There was a Brutus once that would have brook'd
The eternal devil to keep this state of Rome
From falling into scorn and ill repute.

BRUTUS. That you do love me, I am nothing jealous;
What you would work me to, I have some aim:
How I have thought of this and of these times,
I shall recount hereafter; for this present,
I would not, so with love I might entreat you,
Be any further moved. What you have said
I will consider; what you have to say
I will with patience hear, and find a time
Both meet to hear and answer such high things.
Till then, my noble friend, chew upon this:
Brutus had rather be a villager
Than to repute himself a son of Rome
Under these hard conditions as this time
Is like to lay upon us.

CASSIUS. I am glad
That my weak words have struck but thus much show
Of fire from Brutus.

(*Shout. Flourish.*)

BRUTUS. Another shout!

(**CINNA** *comes from the house, in a foul humour.*)

CASSIUS. As she pass by, pluck Cinna by the sleeve
And she will (after her sour fashion) tell you
What hath proceeded worthy note today.

CINNA. You pulled me by the cloak. Would you speak with me?

BRUTUS. Pray, Cinna; tell us what hath chanced to-night,
At Caesar's Lupercal.

CINNA. Why, you were with him, were you not?

BRUTUS. I should not then ask Cinna what had chanced.

CINNA. Why, there was a crown offered him: and being offered him, he put it by with the back of his hand, thus; and then the people fell a-shouting.

BRUTUS. What was the second noise for?

CINNA. Why, for that too.

CASSIUS. They shouted thrice: what was the last cry for?

CINNA. Why, for that too.

BRUTUS. Was the crown offered him thrice?

CINNA. Ay, marry, was't, and he put it by thrice, every time gentler than other, and at every putting-by mine honest neighbours shouted. But, for all that, to my thinking, he would fain have had it. Nay, to my thinking, he was very loath to lay his fingers off it. And when they offered it the third time, the rabblement hooted and clapped their chapped hands and threw up their sweaty night-caps and uttered such a deal of stinking breath because Caesar refused the crown that it had almost choked Caesar; for he swounded and fell down at it: and for mine own part, I durst not laugh, for fear of opening my lips and receiving the bad air.

CASSIUS. But, soft, I pray you: what, did Caesar swound?

CINNA. He fell down in the market-place, and foamed at mouth, and was speechless.

BRUTUS. 'Tis very like: he hath the falling sickness.

CASSIUS. No, Caesar hath it not; but you and I,
And honest Cinna, we have the falling sickness.

CINNA. I know not what you mean by that; but, I am sure, Caesar fell down. If the tag-rag people did not clap him and hiss him, according as he pleased and displeased them, as they use to do the players in the theatre, I am no true Roman.

BRUTUS. What said he when he came unto himself?

CINNA. Marry, before he fell down, when he perceived the common herd was glad he refused the crown, he plucked me ope his bodice and offered them his throat to cut. An I had been a man of any occupation, if I would not have taken him at a word, I would I might go to hell among the rogues. And so he fell. When he came to himself again, he said, if he had done or said any thing amiss, he desired their worships to think it was his infirmity. Three or four wenches, where I stood, cried 'Alas, good soul!' and forgave him with all their hearts: but there's no heed to be taken of them; if Caesar had stabbed their mothers, they would have done no less. Fare you well. There was more foolery yet, if I could remember it.

(*Exit*)

CAESAR. (*Within*) Brutus!

BRUTUS. Anon! For this time I will leave you:
To-morrow, if you please to speak with me,
Come home to me, and I will wait for you.

CASSIUS. I will do so: till then, think of the world.

(*Exit* **BRUTUS**.)

Well, Brutus, thou art loyal; yet, I see,
Thy honourable metal may be wrought
From that it is disposed: therefore it is meet
That noble minds keep ever with their likes;
For who so firm that cannot be seduced?
Caesar doth bear me hard; but he loves Brutus:
If I were Brutus now and he were Cassius,
He should not humour me. I will this night,
In several hands, in at his windows throw,
As if they came from several citizens,
Writings all tending to the great opinion
That Rome holds of his name; wherein obscurely
Caesar's agenda shall be glancèd at:
And after this let Caesar seat him sure;
For we will shake him, or worse days endure.

(*Exit*)

SCENE 3
A hall in Caesar's house.

(**CAESAR** *calls* **BRUTUS** *to him.*)

CAESAR. Come hither, Brute. What is yond gentleman?
BRUTUS. The son and heir of old Tiberius.
CAESAR. What's he that now is going out of door?
BRUTUS. Marry, that, I think, be young Petrucio.
CAESAR. What's he that follows there, that would not dance?
BRUTUS. His name is Romeo, son of Caius Cassius.

(**CAESAR** *cringes at the name.*)

CAESAR. That Cassius has a lean and hungry look;
　　He thinks too much: such men are dangerous.
　　Let me have men about me that are fat;
　　Sleek-headed men and such as sleep o' nights.
BRUTUS. Fear him not, Caesar; he's not dangerous;
　　He is a noble Roman and well given.
CAESAR. Would he were fatter! But I fear him not:
　　Yet if my name were liable to fear,
　　I do not know the man I should avoid
　　So soon as that spare Cassius. He reads much;
　　He is a great observer and he looks
　　Quite through the deeds of men: he loves no plays,
　　As thou dost, Brutus; nor he hears no music;
　　Seldom he smiles, and smiles in such a sort
　　As if he mock'd himself and scorn'd his spirit
　　That could be moved to smile at any thing.
　　Such men as he be never at heart's ease
　　Whiles they behold a merrier than themselves,
　　And therefore are they very dangerous.
　　I rather tell thee what is to be fear'd
　　Than what I fear; for always I am Caesar.
　　But take my right hand, for this ear is deaf,
　　And tell me what thou thinkest of his son.

(*Exeunt*)

(*Enter* CASSIUS, NURSE *and* ROSALINE *the* SOOTH-SAYER.)

CASSIUS. A bears him like a portly gentleman,
And, to say truth, all Roma brags of him
To be a virtuous and well-governed youth.

NURSE. O, he's a lovely boy: an eagle, madam,
Hath not so green, so quick, so fair an eye
As Romeo hath. Beshrew my very heart,
He was the prettiest babe that e'er I nursed—

CASSIUS. I pray thee hold thy peace.

NURSE. Peace, I have done.

ROSALINE. But wherefore do you hold me here so long?
What is the matter?

CASSIUS. Tell me lady Rosaline,
How stands your disposition to be married?

ROSALINE. It is an honour that I dream not of.

CASSIUS. Well, think of marriage now. Thus then in brief:
The valiant Romeo seeks you for his love.

NURSE. A man, young lady, lady, such a man
As all the world—why he's a man of wax.

CASSIUS. The Roman summer hath not such a flower.

NURSE. Nay, he's a flower, in faith, a very flower.

CASSIUS. What say you? Can you love the gentleman?
This night you may behold him at this feast.
Read o'er the volume of young Romeo's face,
And find delight writ there with beauty's pen.
That book in many's eyes doth share the glory,
That in gold clasps locks in the golden story;
So shall you share all that he doth possess,
By having him making yourself no less.

NURSE. No less? Nay, bigger! Women grow by men.

CASSIUS. Speak briefly, can you like of Romeo's love?

ROSALINE. I'll look to like, if looking liking move;

> But no more deep may I endart mine eye
> Than God's consent gives strength to make it fly.

NURSE. Go thy ways, wench; serve God.

(*Exeunt*)

(*Enter* **METELLUS**; *He sees* **CAESAR** *approaching and withdraws.*)

(*Enter* **CAESAR** *and* **ROMEO**, *who takes him by the hand.*)

ROMEO. If I profane with my unworthiest hand
> This holy shrine, the gentle fine is this:
> My lips, two blushing pilgrims, ready stand
> To smooth that rough touch with a tender kiss.

CAESAR. Good pilgrim, you do wrong your hand too much,
> Which mannerly devotion shows in this;
> For saints have hands that pilgrims' hands do touch,
> And palm to palm is holy palmers' kiss.

ROMEO. Have not saints lips, and holy palmers too?

CAESAR. Ay, pilgrim, lips that they must use in prayer.

ROMEO. O, then, dear saint, let lips do what hands do;
> They pray, grant thou, lest faith turn to despair.

CAESAR. Saints do not move, though grant for prayers' sake.

ROMEO. Then move not, while my prayer's effect I take.

(*They kiss.*)

> Thus from my lips, by yours, my sin is purged.

CAESAR. Then have my lips the sin that they have took.

ROMEO. Sin from thy lips? O trespass sweetly urged!
> Give me my sin again.

(*They kiss again. Thunder and lightning.*)

CAESAR. You kiss by the book.

(*Exeunt*)

(**METELLUS** *comes forward.*)

METELLUS. Now old desire doth in his death-bed lie,
> And strange affection gapes to be his heir;

That fair for which love groan'd for and would die,
With noble Julius match'd, is now not fair.
Now Romeo is beloved and loves again,
Belike betwitchèd by the charm of looks,
But to his father's foe he must complain,
And he steal love's sweet bait from fearful hooks.

(*Exit*)

ACT II

SCENE 1
A lane by the wall of Caesar's orchard.

(*Thunder and lightning still. Enter from opposite sides,* CINNA, *with a sword drawn, and* CASSIUS.)

CASSIUS. Good even, Cinna: brought you Caesar home?
Why are you breathless? and why stare you so?

CINNA. Are not you moved, when all the sway of earth
Shakes like a thing unfirm? O Cassius,
I have seen tempests, when the scolding winds
Have rived the knotty oaks, and I have seen
The ambitious ocean swell and rage and foam,
To be exalted with the threatening clouds:
But never till to-night, never till now,
Did I go through a tempest dropping fire.
Either there is a civil strife in heaven,
Or else the world, too saucy with the gods,
Incenses them to send destruction.

CASSIUS. Why, saw you any thing more wonderful?

CINNA. Indeed, I ha' not since put up my sword,
Against the Capitol I met a lion,
Who glared upon me, and went surly by,
Without annoying me: and there were drawn
Upon a heap a hundred ghastly women,
Transformèd with their fear; who swore they saw
Men all in fire walk up and down the streets.
And yesterday the bird of night did sit
Even at noon-day upon the market-place,
Hooting and shrieking. When these prodigies

>   Do so conjointly meet, let not men say
>   'These are their reasons; they are natural;'
>   For, I believe, they are portentous things
>   Unto the climate that they point upon.
> CASSIUS. Indeed, it is a strange-disposèd time:
>   But one may construe things after their fashion,
>   Clean from the purpose of the things themselves.
> CINNA. Good night then, Cassius: this disturbèd sky
>   Is not to walk in. What a night is this!
> CASSIUS. You are dull, Cinna, and those sparks of life
>   That should be in a Roman you do want,
>   Or else you use not. You look pale and gaze
>   And put on fear and cast yourself in wonder,
>   To see the strange impatience of the heavens:
>   But if you would consider the true cause
>   Why all these fires, why all these gliding ghosts,
>   Why all these things change from their ordinance
>   Their natures and preformèd faculties
>   To monstrous quality,—why, you shall find
>   That heaven hath infused them with these spirits,
>   To make them instruments of fear and warning
>   Unto some monstrous state.
>   Now could I, Cinna, name to thee a man
>   Most like this dreadful night,
>   That thunders, lightens, opens graves, and roars
>   As doth the lion in the Capitol,
>   A man no mightier than thyself or me
>   In personal action, yet outrageous grown
>   And fearful, as these strange eruptions are.
> CINNA. 'Tis Caesar that you mean; is it not, Cassius?
> CASSIUS. Let it be who it is: for Romans now
>   Have thews and limbs like to their ancestors;
>   But, woe the while! our fathers' minds are dead,
>   And we are govern'd with our mothers' spirits;
>   Our yoke and sufferance show us womanish.

CINNA. Indeed, they say the senators tomorrow
    Mean to establish Caesar as a king.
CASSIUS. Those that with haste will make a mighty fire
    Begin it with weak straws: what trash is Rome,
    What rubbish and what offal, when it serves
    For the base matter to illuminate
    So vile a thing as Caesar! But, O grief,
    Where hast thou led me? I perhaps speak this
    Before a willing bondmaid; then I know
    My answer must be made. But I am arm'd,
    And dangers are to me indifferent.
CINNA. You speak to Cinna, and to such a one
    That is no fleering tell-tale. Hold, my hand:
    Be factious for redress of all these griefs,
    And I will set this foot of mine as far
    As who goes farthest.
CASSIUS. There's a bargain made.
    Now know you, Cinna, I have moved already
    Some certain of the noblest-minded Romans
    To undergo with me an enterprise
    Of honourable-dangerous consequence;
    And I do know, by this, they stay for me
    In Pompey's porch.
CINNA. O Cassius, if you could
    But win the noble Brutus to our party,
    For he sits high in all his people's hearts:
    And that which would appear offence in us,
    His countenance, like richest alchemy,
    Will change to virtue and to worthiness.
CASSIUS. Come, Cinna, you and I will yet ere day
    See Brutus at his house: three parts of him
    Is ours already, and the man entire
    Upon the next encounter yields him ours.

    (*They see* **ROMEO** *approaching along the orchard wall.*)

ROMEO. Can I go forward when my heart is here?
　　Turn back, dull earth, and find thy centre out.

　(*He climbs the wall, and leaps down within it.*)

CINNA. This, by his voice, should be thy Romeò.

CASSIUS. I wonder that my heavy-hearted son
　　Comes hither. What! is Rosaline about?

CINNA. He ran this way, and leap'd this orchard wall.

CASSIUS. Come, he hath hid himself among these trees,
　　To be consorted with the humorous night:
　　Blind is his love and best befits the dark.

　(*Exeunt*)

SCENE 2
Caesar's orchard.

(*Enter* **ROMEO**.)

ROMEO. They jest at scars that cannot feel the wound.

(**CAESAR** *appears above at a window.*)

But, soft! what light through yonder window breaks?
It is the east, my Julius is the sun.
Arise, fair sun, and kill the envious moon,
Who is already sick and pale with grief,
That thou her man art far more fair than she.
It is my Caesar, O, it is my love!
O, that he knew he were!
He speaks yet he says nothing: what of that?
His eye discourses; I will answer it.
I am too bold, 'tis not to me he speaks:
Two of the fairest stars in all the heaven,
Having some business, do entreat his eyes
To twinkle in their spheres till they return.
See, how he leans his cheek upon his hand!
O, that I were a glove upon that hand,
That I might touch that cheek!

CAESAR. Ay me!

ROMEO. He speaks:

O, speak again, bright angel! for thou art
As glorious to this night, being o'er my head
As is a wingèd messenger of heaven
Unto the white-upturnèd wondering eyes
Of mortals that fall back to gaze on him
When he bestrides the lazy-pacing clouds
And sails upon the bosom of the air.

CAESAR. O Romeo, Romeo! wherefore art thou Romeo?
'tis but thy name that is my enemy;
Thou art thyself, though not a Cassius.
What's Cassius? it is nor hand, nor foot,

Nor arm, nor face, nor any other part
Belonging to a man. O, be some other name!
What's in a name? that which we call a rose
By any other name would smell as sweet;
So Romeo would, were he not Romeo call'd,
Retain that dear perfection which he owes
Without that title. Romeo, doff thy name,
And for that name which is no part of thee
Take all myself.

ROMEO. I take thee at thy word:
Call me but love, and I'll be new baptized;
Henceforth I never will be Romeò.

CAESAR. What man art thou that thus bescreen'd in night
So stumblest on my counsel?

ROMEO. By a name
I know not how to tell thee who I am:
My name, dear saint, is hateful to myself,
Because it is an enemy to thee;
Had I it written, I would tear the word.

CAESAR. My ears have not yet drunk a hundred words
Of that tongue's utterance, yet I know the sound:
Art thou not Romeo son of Cassius?

ROMEO. Neither, fair saint, if either thee dislike.

CAESAR. How camest thou hither, tell me, and wherefore?
The orchard walls are high and hard to climb,
And the place death, considering the hour,
If any of my watchmen found thee here.

ROMEO. With love's light wings did I o'er-perch these walls;
For stony limits cannot hold love out,
And what love can do that dares love attempt;
Therefore thy watchmen are no let to me.

CAESAR. If they do see thee, they will murder thee.

ROMEO. Alack, there lies more peril in thine eye
Than twenty of their swords: look thou but sweet,

And I am proof against their enmity.
CAESAR. I would not for the world they saw thee here.
ROMEO. I have night's cloak to hide me from their sight;
And but thou love me, let them find me here:
My life were better ended by their hate,
Than death prorogued, wanting of thy love.
CAESAR. Thou know'st the mask of night is on my face,
Else would a maiden's blush bepaint my cheek
For that which thou hast heard me speak to-night.
ROMEO. Dost thou love me? I know thou wilt say 'Ay,'
And I will take thy word: yet if thou swear'st,
Thou mayst prove false; at lovers' perjuries
They say, Jove laughs. O gentle Caesar,
If thou dost love, pronounce it faithfully:
Or if thou think'st I am too quickly won,
I'll frown and be perverse and say thee nay,
So thou wilt woo; but else, not for the world.
CAESAR. In truth, fair nightingale, I am too fond,
And therefore thou mayst think my 'havior light:
But trust me, gentleman, I'll prove more true
Than those that have more cunning to be strange.
I should have been more strange, I must confess,
But that thou overheard'st, ere I was ware,
My true love's passion: therefore pardon me,
And not impute this yielding to light love,
Which the dark night hath so discoverèd.
Sweet youth, by yonder blessèd moon I swear
That tips with silver all these fruit-tree tops –
ROMEO. O, swear not by the moon, the inconstant moon,
That monthly changes in her circled orb,
Lest that thy love prove likewise variable.
CAESAR. What shall I swear by?
ROMEO. Do not swear at all;
Or, if thou wilt, swear by thy gracious self,
Which is the god of my idolatry,

And I'll believe thee.

CAESAR. Well, I will not swear,
    Good night, my sweet: although I joy in thee,
    I have no joy of this contract to-night:
    It is too rash, too unadvised, too sudden;
    Too like the lightning, which doth cease to be
    Ere one can say 'It lightens.' Sweet, good night!
    This bud of love, by summer's ripening breath,
    May prove a beauteous flower when next we meet.
    Good night, good night! as sweet repose and rest
    Come to thy heart as that within my breast!

ROMEO. O, wilt thou leave me so unsatisfied?

CAESAR. What satisfaction canst thou have to-night?

ROMEO. The exchange of thy love's faithful vow for mine.

CAESAR. I gave thee mine before thou didst request it:
    And yet I would it were to give again.

ROMEO. Wouldst thou withdraw it? for what purpose, love?

CAESAR. But to be frank, and give it thee again.
    And yet I wish but for the thing I have:
    My bounty is as boundless as the sea,
    My love as deep; the more I give to thee,
    The more I have, for both are infinite.

(*Servant calls within.*)

    I hear some noise within; dear love, adieu!
    Anon, I come! Sweet Romeò, be true.
    Stay but a little, I will come again.

(*Exit, above.*)

ROMEO. O blessèd, blessèd night! I am afeard.
    Being in night, all this is but a dream,
    Too flattering-sweet to be substantial.

(*Re-enter* CAESAR, *above.*)

CAESAR. 'Tis almost morning; I would have thee gone:
    And yet no further than a wanton's bird;
    Who lets it hop a little from her hand,

Like a poor prisoner in his twisted gyves,
And with a silk thread plucks it back again,
So loving-jealous of his liberty.

ROMEO. I would I were thy bird.

CAESAR. Sweet, so would I:
Yet I should kill thee with much cherishing.
Good night, good night! parting is such sweet sorrow,
That I shall say good night till it be morrow.

ROMEO. Sleep dwell upon thine eyes, peace in thy breast!
Would I were sleep and peace, so sweet to rest!
So thrive my soul—

CAESAR. A thousand times good night!

ROMEO. A thousand times the worse, to want thy light.

(*Retiring*)

CAESAR. Love goes toward love, as schoolboys from their books,
But love from love, toward school with heavy looks.
Hist! Romeo, hist! O, for a falconer's voice,
To lure this tassel-gentle back again!

(*Re-enter* **ROMEO**.)

ROMEO. It is my soul that calls upon my name:
How silver-sweet sound lovers' tongues by night,
Like softest music to attending ears!

CAESAR. Romeo!

ROMEO. My dear?

CAESAR. I have forgot why I did call thee back.

ROMEO. Let me stand here till thou remember it.

CAESAR. I shall forget, to have thee still stand there,
Remembering how I love thy company.

ROMEO. And I'll still stay, to have thee still forget,
Forgetting any other home but this.

(**ROMEO** *climbs up to the balcony for a kiss; and they exit into the house.*)

SCENE 3
Brutus's orchard.

(**BRUTUS** *rests on a bench.* **LUCIUS**, *his page, lies asleep with his head on* **BRUTUS**'s *lap.*)

BRUTUS. Boy? Lucius? Fast asleep? It is no matter;
Enjoy the honey-heavy dew of slumber:
Thou hast no figures nor no fantasies,
Which busy care draws in the brains of men;
Therefore thou sleep'st so sound.

(**LUCIUS** *wakes.*)

LUCIUS. Call'd you, my lord?
BRUTUS. Get me a taper in my study, Lucius:
When it is lighted, come and call me here.
LUCIUS. I will, my lord.

(*Exit*)

BRUTUS. It must be by his death: and for my part,
I know no personal cause to spurn at him,
But for the general. He goes too far.
The abuse of greatness is, when it disjoins
Remorse from power: and, to speak truth of Caesar,
I have not known when his affections sway'd
More than his reason. But 'tis a common proof,
That lowliness is young ambition's ladder,
Whereto the climber-upward turns his face;
But when he once attains the upmost round.
He then unto the ladder turns his back,
Looks in the clouds, scorning the base degrees
By which he did ascend. So Caesar may.
Then, lest he may, prevent. And, since the quarrel
Will bear no colour for the thing he is,
Fashion it thus; that what he is, augmented,
Would run to these and these extremities:
And therefore think him as a serpent's egg

Which, hatch'd, would, as his kind, grow mischievous,
And kill him in the shell.

(*Re-enter* **LUCIUS**.)

LUCIUS. The taper burneth in your closet, sir.
Searching the window for a flint, I found
This paper, thus seal'd up; and, I am sure,
It did not lie there when I went to bed.

(*Gives him the letter*)

BRUTUS. Is not to-morrow, boy, the ides of March?

LUCIUS. I know not, sir.

BRUTUS. Look in the calendar, and bring me word.

LUCIUS. I will, sir.

(*Exit*)

(*Thunder and lightning.*)

BRUTUS. The exhalations whizzing in the air
Give so much light that I may read by them.

(*Opens the letter and reads*)

'Brutus, thou sleep'st: awake, and see thyself.
Shall Rome, &c. Speak, strike, redress!
Brutus, thou sleep'st: awake!'
Such instigations have been often dropp'd
Where I have took them up. Am I entreated
To speak and strike? O Rome, I make thee promise:
If the redress will follow, thou receivest
Thy full petition at the hand of Brutus!

(*Re-enter* **LUCIUS**.)

LUCIUS. Sir, March is wasted fourteen days.

(*Knocking within*)

BRUTUS. 'Tis good. Go to the gate; somebody knocks.

(*Exit* **LUCIUS**.)

Since Cassius first did whet me against Caesar,
I have not slept.

Between the acting of a dreadful thing
And the first motion, all the interim is
Like a phantasma, or a hideous dream:
The genius and the mortal instruments
Are then in council; and the state of man,
Like to a little kingdom, suffers then
The nature of an insurrection.

(*Re-enter* **LUCIUS**.)

LUCIUS. Sir, 'tis your brother Cassius at the door,
Who doth desire to see you.
BRUTUS. Is he alone?
LUCIUS. No, sir, there are moe with him.
BRUTUS. Do you know them?
LUCIUS. No, sir; their hats are pluck'd about their ears,
And half their faces buried in their cloaks,
That by no means I may discover them
By any mark of favour.
BRUTUS. Let 'em enter.

(*Exit* **LUCIUS**.)

They are the faction. O conspiracy,
Shamest thou to show thy dangerous brow by night,
When evils are most free? O, then by day
Where wilt thou find a cavern dark enough
To mask thy monstrous visage?

(*Enter the conspirators,* **CASSIUS**, **CINNA**, **METELLUS CIMBER**, *et. al.*)

CASSIUS. I think we are too bold upon your rest:
Good morrow, Brutus; do we trouble you?
BRUTUS. I have been up this hour, awake all night.
Know I these men that come along with you?
CASSIUS. Yes, every one of them, and no one here
But honours you; and every one doth wish
You had but that opinion of yourself
Which every noble Roman bears of you.

BRUTUS. Give me your hands all over, one by one.
CASSIUS. And let us swear our resolution.
BRUTUS. No, not an oath: If not the face of men,
   The sufferance of our souls, the time's abuse;
   If these be motives weak, break off betimes,
   And every man hence to his idle bed.
   So let high-sighted tyranny range on
   Till each man drop by lottery. But if these
   (As I am sure they do) bear fire enough
   To kindle cowards and to steel with valor
   The melting spirits of women, then, countrymen,
   What need we any spur but our own cause,
   To prick us to redress? What needs an oath;
   When every drop of blood a Roman bears
   Is guilty of a several bastardy,
   If he do break the smallest particle
   Of any promise that hath pass'd from him.
CINNA. Shall no man else be touch'd but only Caesar?
CASSIUS. Cinna, well urged: It is not meet that those
   Who share in Caesar's sin share not his fate.
BRUTUS. Our course will seem too bloody, Caius Cassius,
   To cut the head off and then hack the limbs,
   Like wrath in death and envy afterwards;
   Let us be sacrificers, but not butchers, Caius.
   Let's kill him boldly, but not wrathfully;
   Let's carve him as a dish fit for the gods,
   Not hew him as a carcass fit for hounds:
   And let our hearts, as subtle masters do,
   Stir up their servants to an act of rage,
   And after seem to chide 'em. This shall make
   Our purpose necessary and not envious:
   Which so appearing to the common eyes,
   We shall be call'd purgers, not murderers.
CASSIUS. 'Tis time to part. But it is doubtful yet,

Whether Caesar will come forth to-day, or no;
For he is superstitious grown of late,
Quite from the main opinion he held once
Of fantasy, of dreams and ceremonies:
It may be, these apparent prodigies,
The unaccustom'd terror of this night,
And the persuasion of his augurers,
May hold him from the Capitol to-day.

CINNA. Never fear that: if he be so resolved,
I can o'ersway him; for he loves to hear
That unicorns may be betray'd with trees,
And bears with glasses, elephants with holes,
Lions with toils and men with flatterers;
But when I tell him he hates flatterers,
He says he does, being then most flatterèd.
Let me work;
For I can give his humour the true bent,
And I will bring him to the Capitol.

CASSIUS. Nay, we will all of us be there to fetch him.

BRUTUS. By the eighth hour: is that the uttermost?

CINNA. Be that the uttermost, and fail not then.

(*Clock strikes*)

CASSIUS. The clock hath stricken three.

CINNA. 'Tis time to part.

CASSIUS. The morning comes upon 's: we'll leave you, Brutus.
And, friends, disperse yourselves; but all remember
What you have said, and show yourselves true Romans.

BRUTUS. Good gentle friends, look fresh and merrily;
Let not our looks put on our purposes,
But bear it as our Roman actors do,
With untired spirits and formal constancy:
And so good morrow to you every one.

(*Exeunt all but* **BRUTUS**.)

(*Enter* **PORTIA**.)

PORTIA. Brutus, my lord!

BRUTUS. Portia, what mean you? wherefore rise you now?
    It is not for your health thus to commit
    Your weak condition to the raw cold morning.

PORTIA. Nor for yours neither. You've ungently, Brutus,
    Stole from my bed: and yesternight, at supper,
    You suddenly arose, and walk'd about,
    Musing and sighing, with your arms across,
    And when I ask'd you what the matter was,
    You stared upon me with ungentle looks;
    I urged you further; then you scratch'd your head,
    And too impatiently stamp'd with your foot;
    Yet I insisted, yet you answer'd not,
    But, with an angry wafture of your hand,
    Gave sign for me to leave you: so I did;
    Fearing to strengthen that impatience
    Which seem'd too much enkindled, and withal
    Hoping it was but an effect of humour,
    Which sometime hath his hour with every man.
    It will not let you eat, nor talk, nor sleep,
    And could it work so much upon your shape
    As it hath much prevail'd on your condition,
    I should not know you, Brutus. Dear my lord,
    Make me acquainted with your cause of grief.

BRUTUS. I am not well in health, and that is all.

PORTIA. Brutus is wise, and, were he not in health,
    He would embrace the means to come by it.

BRUTUS. Why, so I do. Good Portia, go to bed.

PORTIA. Is Brutus sick? and is it physical
    To walk unbracèd and suck up the humours
    Of the dank morning? What, is Brutus sick,
    And will he steal out of his wholesome bed,
    To dare the vile contagion of the night

And tempt the rheumy and unpurgèd air
To add unto his sickness? No, my Brutus;
You have some sick offence within your mind,
Which, by the right and virtue of my place,
I ought to know of: and, upon my knees,
I charm you, by my once-commended beauty,
By all your vows of love and that great vow
Which did incorporate and make us one,
That you unfold to me, yourself, your half,
Why you are heavy, and what men to-night
Have had to resort to you: for here have been
Some six or seven, who did hide their faces
Even from darkness.

BRUTUS. Kneel not, gentle Portia.

PORTIA. I should not need, if you were gentle Brutus.
Within the bond of marriage, tell me, Brutus,
Is it excepted I should know no secrets
That appertain to you? Am I yourself
But, as it were, in sort or limitation,
To keep with you at meals, comfort your bed,
And talk to you sometimes?
Dwell I but in the suburbs
Of your good pleasure? If it be no more,
Portia is Brutus' harlot, not his wife.

BRUTUS. You are my true and honourable wife,
As dear to me as are the ruddy drops
That visit my sad heart.

PORTIA. If this were true, then should I know this secret.
I grant I am a woman; but withal
A woman that Lord Brutus took to wife:
A woman well-reputed, Cato's daughter.
Think you I am no stronger than my sex,
Being so father'd and so husbanded?
Tell me your counsels, I will not disclose 'em:

I have made strong proof of my constancy,
Giving myself a voluntary wound
Here, in the thigh: can I bear that with patience.
And not my husband's secrets?

BRUTUS. O ye gods,
Render me worthy of this noble wife!

(*A lark sings within*)

Portia, go in awhile;
And by and by thy bosom shall partake
The secrets of my heart. All my engagements
I will construe to thee,
All the charactery of my sad brows:
Leave me with haste.

(*Exit* **PORTIA**.)

ACT III

SCENE 1
Caesar's house.

(*Enter* **ROMEO** *and* **CAESAR** *above, at the window.*)

CAESAR. Wilt thou be gone? it is not yet near day:
It was the nightingale, and not the lark,
That pierced the fearful hollow of thine ear;
Nightly she sings on yon pomegranate-tree:
Believe me, love, it was the nightingale.

ROMEO. It was the lark, the herald of the morn,
No nightingale: look, love, what envious streaks
Do lace the severing clouds in yonder east:
Night's candles are burnt out, and jocund day
Stands tiptoe on the misty mountain tops.
I must be from your chamber gone and home
Before my father's household finds me absent.

CAESAR. Yon light is not day-light, I know it, I:
It is some meteor that the sun exhales,
To be to thee this night a torch-bearer,
And light thee on thy way to Cassius' house:
Therefore stay yet; thou need'st not to be gone.

ROMEO. Let them discover then and cast me out;
I am content, so thou wilt have it so.
I'll say yon grey is not the morning's eye,
'tis but the pale reflex of Cynthia's brow;
Nor that is not the lark, whose notes do beat
The vaulty heaven so high above our heads:
I have more care to stay than will to go:
Come, shame, and welcome! Julius wills it so.

(**CAESAR** *turns away.*)

How is't, my soul? let's talk; it is not day.

CAESAR. It is, it is: hie hence, be gone, away!
It is the lark that sings so out of tune,
Straining harsh discords and unpleasing sharps.
Some say the lark makes sweet division;
This doth not so, for she divideth us.

(*Pulls away from him*)

ROMEO. What mean you, Caesar? think you to walk forth?
You shall not stir out of your bed to-day.
We'll send a messenger to the senate-house:
And he shall say you are not well to-day:
Let me, upon my knee, prevail in this.

CAESAR. But, for thy humour, I will stay at home.

(*Enter* **CINNA.**)

Here's Cinna coming, she shall tell them so.

CINNA. Caesar, all hail! good morrow, worthy Caesar:
I come to fetch you to the senate-house.

CAESAR. And you are come in very happy time,
To bear my greeting to the senators
And tell them that I will not come to-day:
Cannot, is false, and that I dare not, falser:
I will not come to-day: tell them so, Cinna.

ROMEO. Say he is sick.

CAESAR. Shall Caesar send a lie?
Have I in conquest stretch'd mine arm so far,
To be afraid to tell graybeards the truth?
Cinna, go tell them Caesar will not come.

CINNA. Most mighty Caesar, let me know some cause,
Lest I be laugh'd at when I tell them so.

CAESAR. The cause is in my will: I will not come;
That is enough to satisfy the senate.
But for your private satisfaction,

Because I love you, I will let you know:
My Romeo here, my love, stays me at home.
CINNA. Why, may one ask?
ROMEO. I dream'd a dream to-night.
CINNA. And so did I.
ROMEO. Well, what was yours?
CINNA. That dreamers often lie.
ROMEO. In bed asleep, while they do dream things true.
CINNA. O, then, I see Queen Mab hath been with you.
She is the fairies' midwife, and she comes
In shape no bigger than an agate-stone
On the fore-finger of an alderman,
Drawn with a team of little atomies
Athwart men's noses as they lie asleep;
Her wagon-spokes made of long spiders' legs,
The cover of the wings of grasshoppers,
The traces of the smallest spider's web,
The collars of the moonshine's watery beams,
Her whip of cricket's bone, the lash of film,
Her wagoner a small grey-coated gnat,
Her chariot is an empty hazel-nut
Made by the joiner squirrel or old grub,
Time out o' mind the fairies' coachmakers.
And in this state she gallops night by night
Through lovers' brains, and then they dream of love;
O'er courtiers' knees, that dream on court'sies straight,
O'er lawyers' fingers, who straight dream on fees,
O'er ladies' lips, who straight on kisses dream,
Which oft the angry Mab with blisters plagues,
Because their breaths with sweetmeats tainted are:
Sometime she gallops o'er a courtier's nose,
And then dreams he of smelling out a suit;
Sometime she driveth o'er a soldier's neck,
And then dreams he of cutting foreign throats,

Of breaches, ambuscadoes, Spanish blades,
Of healths five-fathom deep; and then anon
Drums in his ear, at which he starts and wakes,
And being thus frighted swears a prayer or two
And sleeps again. This is that very Mab
That plats the manes of horses in the night,
And bakes the elflocks in foul sluttish hairs,
Which once untangled, much misfortune bodes:
This is the hag, when maids lie on their backs,
That presses them and learns them first to bear,
Making them women of good carriage:
This is she—

CAESAR. Peace, noble Cinna, peace!
Thou talk'st of nothing.

CINNA. True, I talk of dreams,
Which are the children of an idle brain,
Begot of nothing but vain fantasy,
Which is as thin of substance as the air
And more inconstant than the wind, who woos
Even now the frozen bosom of the north,
And, being anger'd, puffs away from thence,
Turning his face to the dew-dropping south.

ROMEO. (*to* **CAESAR**) I dreamt to-night I saw your statua,
Which, like a fountain with an hundred spouts,
Did run pure blood: and many lusty Romans
Came smiling, and did bathe their hands in it.

CINNA. And these do you apply for warnings, and portents,
And evils imminent?
This dream is all amiss interpreted;
It was a vision fair and fortunate:
Your statue spouting blood in many pipes,
In which so many smiling Romans bathed,
Signifies that from you great Rome shall suck
Reviving blood, and that great men shall press

For tinctures, stains, relics and cognizance.
This by your Romeo's dream is signified.

CAESAR. And this way have you well expounded it.

CINNA. I have, when you have heard what I can say:
And know it now: the senate have concluded
To give this day a crown to mighty Caesar.
If you shall send them word you will not come,
Their minds may change. Besides, it were a mock
Apt to be render'd, for some one to say
'Break up the senate till another time,
When Caesar's boy shall meet with better dreams.'
Pardon me, Caesar; for my dear dear love
To our proceeding bids me tell you this;
And reason to my love is liable.

CAESAR. How foolish do your fears seem now, sweet Romeo!
I am ashamèd I did yield to them.
Give me my robe, for I will go.

(*Enter* **BRUTUS**, **METELLUS**, **CASSIUS** *and other conspirators.*)

And look where Cassius is come to fetch me.

CASSIUS. Good morrow, Caesar.

CAESAR. Welcome, Cassius.
What, Brutus, are you stirr'd so early too?
What is 't o'clock?

BRUTUS. Caesar, 'tis strucken eight.

CAESAR. Bid them prepare within:
I am to blame to be thus waited for.
Good friends, go in, and taste some wine with me;
And we, like friends, will straightway go together.

(*Exeunt all but* **CASSIUS**, **METELLUS** *and* **ROMEO**.)

CASSIUS. Have I thought long to see this morning's face,
And doth it give me such a sight as this?

ROMEO. Good morrow, father, cousin.

METELLUS. Cotquean!

CASSIUS. Peace!

METELLUS. Signior Romeo, bon jour! there's a French salutation to your French slop.

Come, is the bride ready to go to church?

CASSIUS. Go in, Metellus; I'll be with thee straight.

METELLUS. The pox of such antic, lisping, affecting fantasticoes.

(*Exit*)

ROMEO. Why, is not this better now than groaning for love?

CASSIUS. Holy Saint Francis, what a change is here!
Is Rosaline, whom thou didst love so dear,
So soon forsaken? young men's love then lies
Not truly in their eyes, but in their parts.
Jesu Maria, what a deal of brine
Hath wash'd thy sallow cheeks for Rosaline!
How much salt water thrown away in waste,
To season love, that of it doth not taste!
The sun not yet thy sighs from heaven clears,
Thy old groans ring yet in my ancient ears;
Lo, here upon thy cheek the stain doth sit
Of an old tear that is not wash'd off yet:
If e'er thou wast thyself and these woes thine,
Thou and these woes were all for Rosaline:
And art thou changed? pronounce this sentence then,
Women may hang, for there's no lack of men.

ROMEO. Thou chid'st me oft for loving Rosaline.

CASSIUS. For doting, not for loving, child of mine.

ROMEO. And bad'st me bury love.

CASSIUS. Not in a grave,
To lay one in, some other out to have.

ROMEO. I pray thee, chide not; he whom I love now
Doth grace for grace and love for love allow;
The other did not so.

CASSIUS. And art thou proud? dost thou not count thee blest,
   Unworthy as thou art, that thou hast caught
   So worthy a gentleman to be thy *bridegroom?*
ROMEO. Good father, I beseech you on my knees,
   Hear me with patience but to speak a word.
CASSIUS. Hang thee, young baggage! disobedient wretch!
   I tell thee what: do not call me thy father,
   Nor never after look me in the face:
   Speak not, reply not, do not answer me;
   My fingers itch. 'Sdeath, I scarce thought me blest
   That God had lent me but this only child;
   But now I see this one is one too much,
   And that I have a curse in having him:
   Out on thee, hilding!
ROMEO. May not one speak?
CASSIUS. God's bread! it makes me mad:
   Day, night, hour, tide, time, work, play,
   Alone, in company, still my hope hath been
   To see thee wed: and having therefore raise you
   A gentleman of noble carriage,
   Of fair demesnes, fair wit, and nobly train'd,
   Stuff'd, as they say, with honourable parts,
   Proportion'd as one's thought would wish a man;
   And then to have a wretched puling fool,
   A whining mammet, in his fortune's tender,
   To say 'I will not wed; I cannot love,
   I love a man; I pray you, pardon me.'
   But, as you'll never wed, I'll pardon you:
   Graze where you will, you shall not house with me:
   Look to't, think on't, I do not use to jest.
   Bethink it well; lay hand on heart, advise:
   An you be mine, you'll shirk this wanton's bed;
   An you be not, hang, beg, starve, die in the streets,
   For, by my soul, I'll ne'er acknowledge thee,

Nor what is mine shall never do thee good:
Trust to't, bethink you; I'll not be forsworn.

ROMEO. Is there no pity sitting in the clouds,
That sees into the bottom of my grief?
O, sweet my father, cast me not away!

CASSIUS. Talk not to me, for I'll not speak a word:
Do as thou wilt, for I have done with thee.

(*Exit*)

SCENE 2
Another room in Caesar's house.

(*Enter* **BRUTUS** *and* **CINNA**.)

CINNA. I think it is not meet,
That Romeò, so well beloved of Caesar,
Should outlive Caesar: we shall find of him
A shrewd contriver; and, you know, his means,
If he improve them, may well stretch so far
As to annoy us all: which to prevent,
Let Romeò and Caesar fall together.

(*Enter* **CASSIUS**.)

BRUTUS. Young Romeò is but as a limb of Caesar:
For he can do no more than Caesar's arm
When Caesar's head is off.

CINNA. Yet I fear him;
For in the ingrafted love he bears to Caesar—

CASSIUS. Alas, good Cinna, do not think of him:
If he love Caesar, all that he can do
Is to himself, take thought and die for Caesar:
And that were much he should.

BRUTUS. There is no fear in him; let him not die;
For he will live, and laugh at this hereafter.

(*Exeunt*)

SCENE 3
Romeo's chamber.

(*Enter* **NURSE** *to discover* **ROMEO** *climbing in through a window.*)

ROMEO. Good morrow, nurse.

NURSE. How now, my headstrong! where have you been
 gadding?

ROMEO. Where I have learn'd me to repent the sin
 Of much obedient self-suppression.

NURSE. Young man, it argues a distemper'd head
 So soon to bid good morrow to thy bed:
 Therefore thy earliness doth me assure
 Thou art up-roused by some distemperature;
 Or if not so, then here I hit it right,
 Our Romeo hath not been in bed to-night.

ROMEO. That last is true; the sweeter rest was mine.

NURSE. God pardon sin! wast thou with Rosaline?

ROMEO. With Rosaline, fair gentlewoman? no;
 I have forgot that name, and that name's woe.

NURSE. That's my good boy: but where hast thou been, then?

ROMEO. I'll tell thee, ere thou ask it me again.
 I have been feasting with an enemy,
 Where on a sudden one hath wounded me,
 That's by me wounded: both our remedies
 Within the help of loving physic lies.

NURSE. Be plain, my lad, and homely in thy drift;
 Riddling confession finds but riddling shrift.

ROMEO. Then plainly know my heart's dear love is set
 On noble Julius, for this night we met:
 As mine on his, so his is set on mine;
 And all combined, save what can be combined
 By holy marriage: when and where and how
 We met, we woo'd and made exchange of vow,
 I'll tell thee as we pass; but this I pray,

Come with me to the Capitol to-day.
Now, good sweet nurse,—O Lord, why look'st thou sad?
Thou shamest the happy music of sweet news
To hear it played with still so sour a face.

NURSE. O deadly sin! O rude immodesty!
Now, afore God, I am so vexed that every part about me quivers. Julius Caesar! If he should lead you into a fool's paradise, as they say, it were a very gross kind of behavior, as they say, for you are yet young in the world, and therefore, if he should deal double with you, truly it were an ill thing to be offered to any gentleman, and a very weak dealing. An a' make a mock of you, I'll take him down, an a' were lustier than he is, and twenty such Jacks; and if I cannot, I'll find those that shall. Scurvy knave!
Shame come to Caesar!

ROMEO. Blister'd be thy tongue
For such a wish! he was not born to shame:
Upon his brow shame is ashamed to sit;
For 'tis a throne where honour may be crown'd
Sole monarch of the universal earth.

NURSE. Well, you have made a simple choice; you know not how to choose a man: Caesar! no, not he; though his face be better than any man's, yet his leg excels all men's; and for a hand, and a foot, and a body, though they be not to be talked on, yet they are past compare: he is not the flower of courtesy, but, I'll warrant him, as gentle as a lamb. O, he's a lovely gentleman! Rosaline's a dishclout to him: God mark thee to his grace! were not I thine only nurse, I would say thou hadst suck'd wisdom from thy teat.

ROMEO. Nurse, go with me unto the Capitol;
To see my Julius in the senate-house;
For he went sickly forth: and I would note
What Caesar doth, what suitors press to him.

NURSE. Go, boy, seek happy nights to happy days.

(*Exeunt*)

ACT IV

SCENE 1
A street. Before the Capitol; the Senate sitting above.

(*Enter* **PORTIA**, *disguised with a shawl, reading a paper.*)

PORTIA. "Caesar, beware of Brutus; take heed of Cassius; come not near Casca; have an eye to Cinna, trust not Trebonius: mark well Metellus Cimber: Decius Brutus loves thee not: thou hast wronged Caius Ligarius. There is but one mind in all these, and it is bent against Caesar. If thou beest not immortal, look about you: security gives way to conspiracy. The mighty gods defend thee!"
Here will I stand till Caesar pass along,
And as a suitor will I give him this.
My heart laments that virtue cannot live
Out of the teeth of emulation.
If thou read this, O Caesar, thou mayst live;
If not, the Fates with traitors do contrive.

(*Enter a crowd of people; among them the Soothsayer.*)

(*Flourish. Enter* **CAESAR**, **BRUTUS**, **CASSIUS**, **CINNA**, **METELLUS CIMBER**, *and others.*)

CAESAR. (*To the* **SOOTHSAYER**) The ides of March are come.
SOOTHSAYER. Ay, Caesar; but not gone.
PORTIA. Hail, Caesar! read this schedule.
CINNA. Metellus doth desire you to o'erread,
  At your best leisure, this his humble suit.
PORTIA. O Caesar, read mine first; for mine's a suit
  That touches Caesar nearer: read it, great Caesar.

CAESAR. What touches us ourself shall be last served.
PORTIA. Delay not, Caesar; read it instantly.
CAESAR. What, is the lady mad?
CINNA. Woman, give place.
CASSIUS. What, urge you your agendas in the street? Come to the Capitol.

(**CAESAR** *goes up to the Senate-House, the rest following.*)

SCENE 2
The Senate.

(*Enter* **ROMEO** *and the* **NURSE** *in the gallery.*)

ROMEO. So tedious is this day
　As is the night before some festival
　To an impatient child that hath new robes
　And may not wear them.
　Come, night; come, Julius; come, thou day in night;
　For thou wilt lie upon the wings of night
　Whiter than new snow on a raven's back.
　Come, gentle night, come, loving, black-brow'd night,
　Spread thy close curtain, love-performing night,
　That runaway's eyes may wink and Julius
　Leap to these arms, untalk'd of and unseen.
　Give me my Caesar; and, when he shall die,
　Take him and cut him out in little stars,
　And he will make the face of heaven so fine
　That all the world will be in love with night
　And pay no worship to the garish sun.

NURSE. O, see where he comes.

(*Enter* **CAESAR** *and the others on the floor of the Senate.*
CAESAR *takes his place at the fore, beneath a statue of Pompey.*)

CAESAR. Are we all ready? What is now amiss
　That Caesar and his senate must redress?

BRUTUS. (*Aside to* **CASSIUS**) Where is Metellus Cimber? Let him go,
　And presently prefer his suit to Caesar.

CINNA. He is address'd: press near and second him.

CASSIUS. Cinna, you are the first that rears your hand.

METELLUS CIMBER. Most high, most mighty, and most puissant Caesar,
　Metellus Cimber throws before thy seat
　An humble heart,—

(*Kneeling*)

CAESAR. I must prevent thee, Cimber.
 These couchings and these lowly courtesies
 Might fire the blood of ordinary men,
 And turn pre-ordinance and first decree
 Into the law of children. Be not fond,
 To think that Caesar bears such rebel blood
 That will be thaw'd from the true quality
 With that which melteth fools; I mean, sweet words,
 Low-crookèd court'sies and base spaniel-fawning.
 Thy brother by decree is banishèd:
 If thou dost bend and pray and fawn for him,
 I spurn thee like a cur out of my way.
 Know, Caesar doth not wrong, nor without cause
 Will he be satisfied.

METELLUS CIMBER. Is there no voice more worthy than my own
 To sound more sweetly in great Caesar's ear
 For the repealing of my banish'd brother?

BRUTUS. I kiss thy hand, but not in flattery, Caesar;
 Desiring thee that Flavius Cimber may
 Have an immediate freedom of repeal.

CAESAR. What, Brutus!

CASSIUS. Pardon, Caesar; Caesar, pardon:
 As low as to thy foot doth Cassius fall,
 To beg enfranchisement for Flavius Cimber.

CAESAR. I could be well moved, if I were as you:
 If I could pray to move, prayers would move me:
 But I am constant as the northern star,
 Of whose true-fix'd and resting quality
 There is no fellow in the firmament.
 Let me a little show it, even in this;
 That I was constant Cimber should be banish'd,
 And constant do remain to keep him so.

CINNA. O Caesar,—
CAESAR. Hence! wilt thou lift up Olympus?
CASSIUS. Great Caesar,—
CAESAR. Doth not Cassius bootless kneel?
CINNA. Speak, hands for me!

(**CINNA** *first, then the other Conspirators stab* **CAESAR**. *Finally,* **BRUTUS** *strikes.*)

CAESAR. Et tu, Brute! Then fall, Caesar.

(*Dies*)

ROMEO. Look, look! O heavy day!
 O me, O me! My love, my only life,
 Revive, look up, or I will die with thee!
 Help, help! Call help.
NURSE. Help, ho! they murder Caesar!
ROMEO. Ah, well-a-day! he's dead, he's dead, he's dead!
 We are undone, O gods, we are undone!
 Alack the day! he's dead, he's dead, he's dead!

(*Falls to the ground*)

NURSE. Romeo, arise; Thou wilt be taken. Fly!
CINNA. Victory! Freedom! Vanity is dead!
 Run hence, proclaim, cry it about the streets.

(*Some Citizens flee, among them* **ROMEO**.)

CASSIUS. Some to the common pulpits, and cry out
 'Sanctity, freedom, and morality!'
CINNA. Go to the pulpit, Brutus.
METELLUS CIMBER. And Cassius too.
BRUTUS. People and senators, be not affrighted;
 Fly not; stand stiff: corruption's debt is paid.
CASSIUS. Where is Romeo?
METELLUS CIMBER. Fled to the street amazed:
 Men, wives and children stare, cry out and run
 As it were doomsday.

SCENE 3
Another street.

(*Terrified Citizens rush about in panic. Enter* **ROMEO**.)

ROMEO. O Julius, Julius, the first love I had!
  O beauteous Caesar! honest gentleman!
  That ever I should live to see thee dead!
  Accurs'd, unhappy, wretched, hateful day!
  Most miserable hour that e'er time saw
  In lasting labour of his pilgrimage!
  But one thing to rejoice and solace in,
  And cruel death hath catch'd it from my sight!
  O woe! O woeful, woeful, woeful day!
  Most lamentable day, most woeful day,
  That ever, ever, I did yet behold!
  O day! O day! O day! O hateful day!
  Never was seen so black a day as this:
  O woeful day, O woeful day!
  Beguiled, divorcéd, wrongéd, spited, slain!
  Most detestable death, by thee beguil'd,
  By cruel cruel thee quite overthrown!
  O love! O life! not life, but love in death!
  Despised, distresséd, hated, martyr'd, kill'd!
  Dead art thou! Alack! my Jule is dead;
  And with my love my joys are buriéd.

(*Enter* **NURSE**.)

NURSE. Stand up, stand up; stand, and you be a man:
  For Julius's sake, for his sake, rise and stand;
  Why should you fall into so deep an O?
ROMEO. O honey nurse! he's dead, deceased, he's dead!
  That gallant spirit hath aspired the clouds,
  Which too untimely here did scorn the earth.
NURSE. Thou hast amazed me: by my holidam,
  I thought thy disposition better temper'd.

What, wilt thou wash him from his grave with tears?
An if thou couldst, thou couldst not make him live;
Therefore, have done: some grief shows much of love;
But much of grief shows still some want of wit.

ROMEO. Then I'll be brief.

(*Snatching up his dagger*)

O happy dagger!
This is thy sheath; there rust, and let me die.

(*He tries to stab himself; the* **NURSE** *prevents him.*)

NURSE. What mean you, Romeo? Hold thy desperate hand:
Art thou a man? thy form cries out thou art:
Thy tears are womanish; thy wild acts denote
The unreasonable fury of a beast:
Unseemly woman in a seeming man!
Or ill-beseeming beast in seeming both!
But, like a misbehaved and sullen wench,
Thou pout'st upon thy fortune and thy love:
Fie, fie, thou shamest thy shape, thy love, thy wit;
Take heed, take heed, for 'tis dishonourable!

(**ROMEO** *falls silent.*)

ROMEO. Speakest thou from thy heart?
NURSE. And from my soul too;
Or else beshrew them both.
ROMEO. Amen!
NURSE. What?
ROMEO. Well, thou hast comforted me marvellous much.
Go back: and tell Lord Brutus I am coming
In meek submission there to be resolved.
NURSE. Good gentle youth—
ROMEO. Leave me, and do the thing I bid thee do.
Commend me to Lord Brutus. Romeo is coming.
NURSE. Marry, I will.

(*Exit*)

SCENE 4
The Senate.

(**BRUTUS**, **CASSIUS**, **CINNA** *and Conspirators, as before, and* **CAESAR** *dead.*)

BRUTUS. Fates, we will know your pleasures:
   That we shall die, we know; 'tis but the time
   And drawing days out, that men stand upon.
CASSIUS. Why, he that cuts off twenty years of life
   Cuts off so many years of fearing death.
BRUTUS. Grant that, and then is death a benefit:
   So are we Caesar's friends, that have abridged
   His time of fearing death. Stoop, Romans, stoop,
   And let us bathe our hands in Caesar's blood
   Up to the elbows, and besmear our swords:
   Then walk we forth, even to the market-place,
   And, waving our red weapons o'er our heads,
   Let's all cry 'Peace, freedom and liberty!'
CASSIUS. Stoop, then, and wash. How many ages hence
   Shall this our lofty scene be acted over
   In states unborn and accents yet unknown!
BRUTUS. How many times shall Caesar bleed in sport,
   That now on Pompey's basis lies along
   No worthier than the dust!
CASSIUS. So oft as that shall be,
   So often shall the knot of us be call'd
   The men that gave their country dignity.

   (*Enter* **NURSE**.)

BRUTUS. Soft! who comes here? A friend of Romeò's.
NURSE. Thus, Brutus, did my master bid me kneel:
   And, being prostrate, thus he bade me say:
   Brutus is noble, wise, valiant, and honest;
   Caesar was mighty, bold, royal, and loving:
   Say I love Brutus, and I honour him;

> Say I fear'd Caesar, honour'd him and loved him.
> If Brutus will vouchsafe that Romeò
> May safely come to him, and be resolvèd
> How Caesar hath deserved to lie in death,
> Then Romeò shall not love Caesar dead
> So well as Brutus living; but will follow
> The fortunes and affairs of noble Brutus. Thorough the hazards of this untrod state
> With all true faith. So says my master Romeo.

BRUTUS. Tell him, so please him come unto this place,
> He shall be satisfied; and, by my honour,
> Depart untouch'd.

(*Re-enter* **ROMEO**.)

> But here comes Romeò.

ROMEO. I know not, gentlemen, what you intend,
> Who else must be let blood, who else is rank:
> If I myself, there is no hour so fit
> As Caesar's death hour, nor no instrument
> Of half that worth as those your swords, made rich
> With the most noble blood of all this world.
> Now, whilst your purpled hands do reek and smoke,
> Fulfil your pleasure. Live a thousand years,
> I shall not find myself so apt to die.

CASSIUS. O Romeò, beg not your death of us.

BRUTUS. Though now we must appear bloody and cruel,
> As, by our hands and this our present act,
> You see we do, yet see you but our hands
> And this the bleeding business they have done:
> Our hearts you see not; they are pitiful;
> And pity to the general wrong of Rome
> Hath done this deed on Caesar. For your part,
> To you our swords have leaden points, good Romeo:
> Our arms, in strength of malice, and our hearts
> Of brothers' temper, do receive you in

With all kind love, good thoughts, and reverence.
Only be patient till we have appeased
The multitude, beside themselves with fear,
And then we will deliver you the cause,
Why I, that did love Caesar when I struck him,
Have thus proceeded.

ROMEO. I doubt not of your wisdom.
Let each man render me his bloody hand:
First, Marcus Brutus, will I shake with you;
Next, valiant Cinna, do I take your hand;
Now, cousin, good Metellus, yours;
Though last, not last in love, yours, Caius Cassius.
Gentle friends all,—Alas, what shall I say?
My credit now stands on such slippery ground,
That one of two bad ways you must conceit me,
Either a coward or a flatterer.
That I did love thee, Caesar, O, 'tis true:
If then thy spirit look upon us now,
Shall it not grieve thee dearer than thy death,
To see thy Romeò making his peace,
Shaking the bloody fingers of thy foes,
Most noble! in the presence of thy corse?
Had I as many eyes as thou hast wounds,
Weeping as fast as they stream forth thy blood,
It would become me better than to close
In terms of friendship with thine enemies.
Pardon me, Julius! Here wast thou bay'd, brave hart;
Here didst thou fall; and here thy hunters stand,
Sign'd in thy spoil, and crimson'd in thy lethe.
O world, thou wast the forest to this hart;
And this, indeed, O world, the heart of thee.
How like a deer, strucken by many princes,
Dost thou here lie!

CASSIUS. O Romeò,—

ROMEO. Pardon me, Caius Cassius:
>The enemies of Caesar shall say this;
>Then, in a friend, it is cold modesty.

CINNA. I blame you not for praising Caesar so;
>But what compact mean you to have with us?
>Will you be prick'd in number of our friends;
>Or shall we on, and not depend on you?

ROMEO. Friends am I with you all and love you all,
>Upon this hope, that you shall give me reasons
>Why and wherein Caesar was dangerous.

BRUTUS. Our reasons are so full of good regard
>That were you, Romeò, the son of Caesar,
>You should be satisfied.

ROMEO. That's all I seek:
>And am moreover suitor that I may
>Produce his body to the market-place;
>And in the pulpit, as becomes a friend,
>Speak in the order of his funeral.

BRUTUS. You shall, good Romeo.

CASSIUS. Brutus, a word with you.
>(*Aside to* **BRUTUS**) You know not what you do: do not consent
>That Romeò speak in his funeral:
>Know you how much the people may be moved
>By that which he will utter?

BRUTUS. By your pardon;
>I will myself into the pulpit first,
>And show the reason of our Caesar's death:
>What Romeo there shall speak, I will protest
>He speaks by leave and by permission,
>And that we are contented Caesar shall
>Have all true rites and lawful ceremonies.
>It shall advantage more than do us wrong.

CASSIUS. I know not what may fall; I like it not.

BRUTUS. Good Romeò, here, take you Caesar's body.
  You shall not in your funeral speech blame us,
  But speak all good you can devise of Caesar,
  And say you do't by our permission;
  Else shall you not have any hand at all
  About his funeral: and you shall speak
  In the same pulpit whereto I am going,
  After my speech is ended.
ROMEO. Be it so.
  I do desire no more.
BRUTUS. Prepare the body then, and follow us.

  (*Exeunt all but* **ROMEO**.)

ROMEO. O, pardon me, thou bleeding piece of earth,
  That I am meek and gentle with these butchers!
  Thou art the ruins of the noblest man
  That ever lived in the tide of times.
  Woe to the hand that shed this costly blood!
  Over thy wounds now do I prophesy,
  (Which, like dumb mouths, do ope their ruby lips,
  To beg the voice and utterance of my tongue)
  A curse shall light upon the limbs of men;
  Domestic fury and fierce civil strife
  Shall cumber all the parts of Italy;
  Blood and destruction shall be so in use
  And dreadful objects so familiar
  That mothers shall but smile when they behold
  Their infants quarter'd with the hands of war;
  All pity choked with custom of fell deeds:
  And Caesar's spirit, ranging for revenge,
  With Ate by his side come hot from hell,
  Shall in these confines with a monarch's voice
  Cry 'Havoc,' and let slip the dogs of war;
  That this foul deed shall smell above the earth
  With carrion men, groaning for burial.

  (*Exit with* **CAESAR**'s *body.*)

SCENE 5
The Forum.

(*Enter* **BRUTUS** *and* **CASSIUS**, *and a throng of Citizens.*)

CITIZENS. We will be satisfied; let us be satisfied.

BRUTUS. Then follow me, and give me audience, friends.
Those that will hear me speak, let 'em stay here;
And public reasons shall be renderèd
Of Caesar's death.

FIRST CITIZEN. I will hear Brutus speak.

(**BRUTUS** *goes into the pulpit.*)

THIRD CITIZEN. The noble Brutus is ascended: silence!

BRUTUS. Be patient till the last.

Romans, countrymen, and lovers! hear me for my cause, and be silent, that you may hear: believe me for mine honour, and have respect to mine honour, that you may believe: censure me in your wisdom, and awake your senses, that you may the better judge. If there be any in this assembly, any dear friend of Caesar's, to him I say, that Brutus' love to Caesar was no less than his. If then that friend demand why Brutus rose against Caesar, this is my answer: Not that I loved Caesar less, but that I loved Rome more. Had you rather Caesar were living and die all slaves, than that Caesar were dead, to live all free men? As Caesar loved me, I weep for him; as he was fortunate, I rejoice at it; as he was valiant, I honour him: but, as he was ambitious, I slew him. There is tears for his love; joy for his fortune; honour for his valour; and death for his ambition. Who is here so base that would be a bondman? If any, speak; for him have I offended. Who is here so rude that would not be a Roman? If any, speak; for him have I offended. Who is here so vile that will not love his country? If any, speak; for him have I offended. I pause for a reply.

ALL. None, Brutus, none.

BRUTUS. Then none have I offended. I have done no more to Caesar than you shall do to Brutus. The question of his death is enrolled in the Capitol; his glory not extenuated, wherein he was worthy, nor his offences enforced, for which he suffered death.

(*Enter* **ROMEO** *and others, with* **CAESAR**'s *body.*)

Here comes his body, mourned by noble Romeo: who, though he had no hand in his death, shall receive the benefit of his dying, a peace in the commonwealth; as which of you shall not? With this I depart: that, as I slew my best lover for the good of Rome, I have the same dagger for myself, when it shall please my country to need my death.

ALL. Live, Brutus! live, live!

FIRST CITIZEN. Bring him with triumph home unto his house.

SECOND CITIZEN. Give him a statue with his ancestors.

THIRD CITIZEN. Let him be Caesar.

FOURTH CITIZEN. Caesar's better parts
Shall be crown'd in Brutus.

FIRST CITIZEN. We'll bring him to his house with shouts and clamours.

BRUTUS. My countrymen,—

SECOND CITIZEN. Peace, silence! Brutus speaks.

FIRST CITIZEN. Peace, ho!

BRUTUS. Good countrymen, let me depart alone,
And, for my sake, stay here with Romeò:
Do grace to Caesar's corpse, and grace his speech
Tending to Caesar's glories; which young Romeo,
By our permission, is allow'd to make.
I do entreat you, not a man depart,
Save I alone, till Romeò have spoke.

(*Exit*)

FIRST CITIZEN. Stay, ho! and let us hear this Romeò.

THIRD CITIZEN. Let him go up into the public chair;

We'll hear him. Noble Romeò, go up.

ROMEO. For Brutus' sake, I am beholding to you.

(**ROMEO** *goes into the pulpit.*)

FOURTH CITIZEN. What does he say of Brutus?

THIRD CITIZEN. He says, for Brutus' sake,
He finds himself beholding to us all.

FOURTH CITIZEN. 'Twere best he speak no harm of Brutus here.

FIRST CITIZEN. This Caesar was a tyrant.

THIRD CITIZEN. Nay, that's certain:
We are blest that Rome is rid of him.

SECOND CITIZEN. Peace! let us hear what Romeò can say.

ROMEO. You gentle Romans,—

CITIZENS. Peace, ho! let us hear him.

ROMEO. Friends, Romans, countrymen, lend me your ears;
I come to bury Caesar, not to praise him.
The evil that men do lives after them;
The good is oft interrèd with their bones;
So let it be with Caesar. The noble Brutus. Hath told you Caesar was ambitious:
If it were so, it was a grievous fault,
And grievously hath Caesar answer'd it.
Here, under leave of Brutus and the rest
(For Brutus is an honourable man;
So are they all, all honourable men)
Come I to speak in Caesar's funeral.
He was my love, faithful and just to me:
But Brutus says he was ambitious;
And Brutus is an honourable man.
He hath brought many captives home to Rome
Whose ransoms did the general coffers fill:
Did this in Caesar seem ambitious?
When that the poor have cried, Caesar hath wept:
Ambition should be made of sterner stuff:

Yet Brutus says he was ambitious;
And Brutus is an honourable man.
You all did see that on the Lupercal
they thrice presented him a kingly crown,
Which he did thrice refuse: was this ambition?
Yet Brutus says he was ambitious;
And, sure, he is an honourable man.
I speak not to disprove what Brutus spoke,
But here I am to speak what I do know.
You all did love him once, not without cause:
What cause withholds you then, to mourn for him?
O judgment! thou art fled to brutish beasts,
And men have lost their reason. Bear with me;
My heart is in the coffin there with Caesar,
And I must pause till it come back to me.

FIRST CITIZEN. Methinks there is much reason in his sayings.

SECOND CITIZEN. If thou consider rightly of the matter,
Caesar has had great wrong.

THIRD CITIZEN. Has he, masters?
I fear there will a worse come in his place.

FOURTH CITIZEN. Mark'd ye his words? He would not take the crown;
Therefore 'tis certain he was not ambitious.

FIRST CITIZEN. If it be found so, some will dear abide it.

SECOND CITIZEN. Poor soul! his eyes are red as fire with weeping.

THIRD CITIZEN. There's not a nobler man in Rome than Romeo.

FOURTH CITIZEN. Now mark him, he begins again to speak.

ROMEO. But yesterday the word of Caesar might
Have stood against the world; now lies he there.
And none so poor to do him reverence.
O masters, if I were disposed to stir

Your hearts and minds to mutiny and rage,
  I should do Brutus wrong, and Cassius wrong,
  Who, you all know, are honourable men:
  I will not do them wrong; I rather choose
  To wrong the dead, to wrong myself and you,
  Than I will wrong such honourable men.

FOURTH CITIZEN. They were traitors: honourable men!

SECOND CITIZEN. They were villains, murderers!

ROMEO. Then make a ring about the corpse of Caesar,
  And let me show you that shall make you weep.

FOURTH CITIZEN. A ring; stand round.

FIRST CITIZEN. Stand from the hearse, stand from the body.

ROMEO. If you have tears, prepare to shed them now.
  You all do know this mantle Caesar wore:
  Look, in this place ran Cassius' dagger through:
  See what a rent the envious Cinna made:
  Through this the well-belovèd Brutus stabb'd;
  And as he pluck'd his cursèd steel away,
  Mark how the blood of Caesar follow'd it,
  As rushing out of doors, to be resolved
  If Brutus so unkindly knock'd, or no;
  For Brutus, as you know, was Caesar's angel:
  Judge, O you gods, how dearly Caesar loved him!
  This was the most unkindest cut of all;
  For when the noble Caesar saw him stab,
  Ingratitude, more strong than traitors' arms,
  Quite vanquish'd him: then burst his mighty heart;
  And, in his mantle muffling up his face,
  Even at the base of Pompey's statua,
  Which all the while ran blood, great Caesar fell.
  O, what a fall was there, my countrymen!
  Then I, and you, and all of us fell down,
  Whilst bloody treason flourish'd over us.

O, now you weep; and, I perceive, you feel
The dint of pity: these are gracious drops.
Kind souls, what, weep you when you but behold
Our Caesar's vesture wounded? Look you here,
Here is himself, marr'd, as you see, with traitors.

FIRST CITIZEN. O piteous spectacle!

SECOND CITIZEN. O noble Caesar!

THIRD CITIZEN. O woeful day!

FOURTH CITIZEN. O traitors, villains!

FIRST CITIZEN. O most bloody sight!

SECOND CITIZEN. We will be revenged.

ALL. Revenge! About! Seek! Burn! Fire! Kill! Slay! Let not a traitor live!

ROMEO. Stay, countrymen.

FIRST CITIZEN. Peace there! hear the noble Romeo.

SECOND CITIZEN. We'll hear him, we'll follow him, we'll die with him.

ROMEO. Good friends, sweet friends, let me not stir you up
To such a sudden flood of mutiny.
They that have done this deed are honourable:
And will, no doubt, with reasons answer you.
I come not, friends, to steal away your hearts:
I am no orator, as Brutus is;
For I have neither wit, nor words, nor worth,
Action, nor utterance, nor the power of speech,
To stir men's blood: I only speak right on;
I tell you that which you yourselves do know;
Show you sweet Caesar's wounds, poor poor dumb mouths,
And bid them speak for me: but were I Brutus,
And Brutus Romeò, there were a Romeo.
Would ruffle up your spirits and put a tongue
In every wound of Caesar that should move
The stones of Rome to rise and mutiny.

ALL. We'll mutiny.

FIRST CITIZEN. We'll burn the house of Brutus.

THIRD CITIZEN. Away, then! come, seek the conspirators.

SECOND CITIZEN. Most noble Caesar! We'll revenge his death.

THIRD CITIZEN. O royal Caesar!

FIRST CITIZEN. Come, away, away!
We'll burn his body in the holy place,
And with the brands fire the traitors' houses.
Take up the body.

SECOND CITIZEN. Go fetch fire.

THIRD CITIZEN. Pluck down benches.

FOURTH CITIZEN. Pluck down forms, windows, any thing.

(*Exeunt Citizens with the body.*)

ROMEO. Now let it work. Mischief, thou art afoot,
Take thou what course thou wilt.

(*Enter* **NURSE**.)

How now, good nurse!

NURSE. I hear them say, Brutus and Cassius
Are rid like madmen through the gates of Rome.

ROMEO. Belike they had some notice of the people,
How I had moved them. Come, we must away.

(*Exeunt*)

ACT V

SCENE 1
A street.

(*Enter* **CINNA THE POET**.)

CINNA THE POET. I dreamt to-night that I did feast with Caesar,
And things unlucky charge my fantasy:
I have no will to wander forth of doors,
Yet something leads me forth.

(*Enter Citizens.*)

FIRST CITIZEN. What is your name?

SECOND CITIZEN. Whither are you going?

THIRD CITIZEN. Where do you dwell?

FOURTH CITIZEN. Are you a married woman or a maid?

SECOND CITIZEN. Answer every man directly.

FIRST CITIZEN. Ay, and briefly.

FOURTH CITIZEN. Ay, and wisely.

THIRD CITIZEN. Ay, and truly, you were best.

CINNA THE POET. What is my name? Whither am I going? Where do I dwell? Am I a married woman or a maid? Then, to answer every man directly and briefly, wisely and truly: wisely I say, I am yet a maid.

SECOND CITIZEN. That's as much as to say, they are fools that marry: you'll bear me a bang for that, I fear. Proceed; directly.

CINNA THE POET. Directly, I am going to Caesar's funeral.

FIRST CITIZEN. As a friend or an enemy?

CINNA THE POET. As a friend.

SECOND CITIZEN. That matter is answered directly.

FOURTH CITIZEN. For your dwelling; briefly.

CINNA THE POET. Briefly, I dwell by the Capitol.

THIRD CITIZEN. Your name, now, truly.

CINNA THE POET. Truly, my name is Cinna.

FIRST CITIZEN. Tear her to pieces; she's a conspirator.

CINNA THE POET. I am Cinna the poet, I am Cinna the poet.

FOURTH CITIZEN. Tear her for her bad verses, tear her for her bad verses.

CINNA THE POET. I am not Cinna the conspirator.

FOURTH CITIZEN. It is no matter, her name's Cinna; pluck but her name out of her heart, and turn her going.

THIRD CITIZEN. Tear her, tear her! Come, brands ho! fire-brands: to Brutus', to Cassius'; burn all: some to Decius' house, and some to Cimber's; some to Ligarius': away, go!

(*Exeunt*)

SCENE 2
The plains of Philippi. The field of battle.

(*Sounds of battle. Alarum. Enter fighting, Soldiers of both armies; then* **BRUTUS**, **CINNA** *and* **LUCIUS**.)

BRUTUS. Come, poor remains of friends, rest on this rock.

CINNA. Metellus show'd the torch-light, but, my lord,
He came not back: he is or ta'en or slain.

(*Low alarums.*)

BRUTUS. Thou seest the world, good Cinna, how it goes;
Our enemies have beat us to the pit:
It is more worthy to leap in ourselves,
Than tarry till they push us.

(*Alarum still.*)

CINNA. Fly, fly, my lord; there is no tarrying here.
Fly further off.

(*Exit*)

BRUTUS. Yet, countrymen, O, yet hold up your heads!

(*Loud alarum. Exeunt, fighting.*)

SCENE 3
Another part of the battlefield.

(*Sounds of battle. Alarums. Soldiers flee. Enter* **METEL-LUS CIMBER**, *injured, and* **CASSIUS**, *who slays one of the retreating soldiers.*)

CASSIUS. O, look, Metellus, look, the villains fly!
Myself have to mine own turn'd enemy:
This ensign here of mine was turning back;
I slew the coward, and did take it from him.

METELLUS CIMBER. O Cassius, now our soldiers fall to spoil,
Whilst we by enemies are all enclosed.

Enter **CINNA**.

CINNA. Fly further off, my lord, fly further off;
The enemy is in your tents, my lord
Fly, therefore, noble Cassius, fly far off.

(*Exeunt*)

SCENE 4
A street in Rome.

(*The sounds of battle further off now. Enter* **ROMEO**, *with a letter, and the* **NURSE**.)

ROMEO. These many, then, shall die; their names are prick'd.

NURSE. Your father too must die? consent you, Romeo?

ROMEO. He shall not live; look, with a spot I damn him.
We must do so: for we are at the stake,
And bay'd about with many enemies;
And some that smile have in their hearts, I fear,
Millions of mischiefs. Therefore, take these letters,
And see the names proclaimed in common pulpits.
This last is for my father, Caius Cassius.
O, nurse, if I could find out but a man
To mix a poison, I would season it;
That Cassius should, upon receipt thereof,
Soon sleep in grief.

(**ROMEO** *starts to hand her the letter, then takes it back.*)

O mischief, thou art swift
To enter in the thoughts of desperate men!
I do remember an apothecary,
And hereabouts he dwells, which late I noted
In tatter'd weeds, with overwhelming brows,
Culling of simples; meagre were his looks,
Sharp misery had worn him to the bones.
Noting this penury, to myself I said
'An if a man did need a poison now,
Here lives a caitiff wretch would sell it him.'
O, this same thought did but forerun my need;
And this same needy man must sell it me.

NURSE. I do beseech you, sir, have patience:
Your looks are pale and wild, and do import
Some misadventure.

ROMEO. Tush, thou art deceived:
    I prithee, nurse, run to the Capitol;
    Stay not to answer me, but get thee gone:
    Why dost thou stay? Begone!

NURSE. Well, I will hie,
    And so bestow these papers as you bade me.

    (*Exit*)

    (**ROMEO** *goes to the door of a certain shop.*)

As I remember, this should be the house.
Being holiday, the beggar's shop is shut.
What, ho! apothecary!

    (*Enter* **APOTHECARY**.)

APOTHECARY. Who calls so loud?

ROMEO. Come hither, man. I see that thou art poor:
    Hold, there is forty ducats: let me have
    A dram of poison, such soon-speeding gear
    As will disperse itself through all the veins
    That the life-weary taker may fall dead
    And that the trunk may be discharged of breath
    As violently as hasty powder fired
    Doth hurry from the fatal cannon's womb.

APOTHECARY. Such mortal drugs I have; but Roman law
    Is death to any he that utters them.

ROMEO. Art thou so bare and full of wretchedness,
    And fear'st to die? famine is in thy cheeks,
    Need and oppression starveth in thine eyes,
    Contempt and beggary hangs upon thy back;
    The world is not thy friend nor the world's law;
    The world affords no law to make thee rich;
    Then be not poor, but break it, and take this.

APOTHECARY. My poverty, but not my will, consents.

ROMEO. I pay thy poverty, and not thy will.

APOTHECARY. Put this in any liquid thing you will,

And whoso drink it, if he had the strength
Of twenty men, it would dispatch him straight.
ROMEO. There is thy gold, worse poison to men's souls,
Doing more murders in this loathsome world,
Than these poor compounds that thou mayst not sell.
I sell thee poison; thou hast sold me none.
Farewell: buy food, and get thyself in flesh.

(*Exeunt*)

SCENE 5
Camp near Sardis. Brutus's tent.

(**BRUTUS** *in his tent, with Soldiers and* **LUCIUS**. *Enter* **CINNA** *with some letters.*)

BRUTUS. Go, bid the commanders
Prepare to lodge their companies to-night.

(*Exeunt two Soldiers.*)

CINNA. Lord Brutus, I have here receivèd letters,
That by proscription and bills of outlawry,
Has Romeo in our absence put to death
An hundred senators. Cicero being one.

BRUTUS. Cicero one!

CINNA. Cicero is dead,
And by that order of proscription.

BRUTUS. Have you had letters from my wife, good Cinna?
Now, as you are a Roman, tell me true.

CINNA. Then like a Roman bear the truth I tell:
For certain she is dead, and by strange manner.

(**CINNA** *gives him the letter;* **BRUTUS** *reads.*)

BRUTUS. Why, farewell, Portia. I am fortune's fool.

(*Drum. Enter* **CASSIUS** *and his powers.*)

CASSIUS. Most noble brother, you have done me wrong.

BRUTUS. Judge me, you gods! wrong I mine enemies?
And, if not so, how should I wrong a brother?

CASSIUS. That you have wrong'd me doth appear in this:
You have condemn'd and noted Lucius Pella
For taking bribes here of the Sardians;
Wherein my letters, praying on his side,
Because I knew the man, were slighted off.

BRUTUS. You wronged yourself to write in such a case.

CASSIUS. In such a time as this it is not meet
That every nice offence should bear his comment.

BRUTUS. Let me tell you, Cassius, you yourself
    Are much condemn'd to have an itching palm;
    To sell and mart your offices for gold
    To undeservers.

CASSIUS. I an itching palm!
    You know that you are Brutus that speak this,
    Or, by the gods, this speech were else your last.

BRUTUS. The name of Cassius honours this corruption,
    And chastisement doth therefore hide his head.

CASSIUS. Chastisement!

BRUTUS. Remember March, the ides of March remember:
    Did not great Julius bleed for justice' sake?
    What villain touch'd his body, that did stab,
    And not for justice? What, shall one of us
    That struck the foremost man of all this world
    But for supporting robbers, shall we now
    Contaminate our fingers with base bribes,
    And sell the mighty space of our convictions
    For so much trash as may be graspèd thus?

CASSIUS. O ye gods, ye gods! must I endure all this?
    Do not presume too much upon my love;
    I may do that I shall be sorry for.

BRUTUS. You have done that you should be sorry for.
    There is no terror, Cassius, in your threats,
    For I am arm'd so strong in honesty
    That they pass by me as the idle wind,
    Which I respect not; for, from this day forth,
    I'll use you for my mirth, yea, for my laughter,
    When you are covetous.

CASSIUS. There is my dagger,
    And here my naked breast; within, a heart
    Dearer than Plutus' mine, richer than gold:
    If that thou be'st a Roman, take it forth;
    Strike, as thou didst at Caesar; for, I know,

When thou didst hate him worst, thou lovedst him better
Than ever thou lovedst Cassius.

BRUTUS. Sheathe your dagger:
Urge me no more, I shall forget myself;
Have mind upon your health, tempt me no further.
Portia is dead.

CASSIUS. Ha! Portia!

BRUTUS. She is dead.

CASSIUS. How 'scaped I killing when I cross'd you so?

BRUTUS. Lucius! My gown. Give me a bowl of wine.

(*Exit* **LUCIUS**.)

CASSIUS. O insupportable and touching loss!
Upon what sickness?

BRUTUS. Impatient of my absence,
And grief that Romeo and our enemies
Have made themselves so strong: for with her death
That tidings came; with this she fell distract,
And, her attendants absent, swallow'd fire.

CASSIUS. And died so?

BRUTUS. Even so.

CASSIUS. O ye immortal gods!

BRUTUS. Speak no more of her. Farewell, good Cassius.

CASSIUS. There is no more to say?

BRUTUS. No more. Good night:
And whether we shall meet again I know not.

CASSIUS. If not, why then this parting was well made.

(*Re-enter* **LUCIUS**, *with wine and taper.*)

BRUTUS. In this I bury all remembrance, Cassius.

(**BRUTUS** *drinks.* **CASSIUS** *departs from him.*)

CASSIUS. O Julius Caesar, thou art mighty yet!
Thy spirit walks abroad and turns our friends
Against our common interests.

(*Exit*)

(*Enter the Ghost of* **CAESAR**.)

BRUTUS. How ill this taper burns! Ha! who comes here?
I think it is the weakness of mine eyes
That shapes this monstrous apparition.
It comes upon me. Art thou any thing?
Art thou some god, some angel, or some devil,
That makest my blood cold and my hair to stare?
Speak to me what thou art.

GHOST. Thy evil spirit, Brutus.

BRUTUS. Why comest thou?

GHOST. To tell thee thou shalt see me yet ere morning.

BRUTUS. Well; then I shall see thee again?

GHOST. Ay, this very night.

BRUTUS. Why, I will see thee then to-night.

(*Exit* **GHOST**.)

Now I have taken heart thou vanishest:
Ill spirit, I would hold more talk with thee.
Lucius, awake!

LUCIUS. My lord?

BRUTUS. Didst thou dream, Lucius, that thou so criedst out?

LUCIUS. My lord, I do not know that I did cry.

BRUTUS. Yes, that thou didst: didst thou see any thing?

LUCIUS. Nothing, my lord.

BRUTUS. Go and commend me to my brother Cassius;
Tell him that I must hie me home to Rome.
There lies one dead that I must speak withal.

LUCIUS. It shall be done, my lord.

(*Exeunt*)

SCENE 6
Rome. A churchyard. In it, the tomb of Caesar.

(*Far off trumpets sound a retreat and the distant sound of battle begins to subside; Enter* **ROMEO**.)

ROMEO. If I may trust the flattering truth of sleep,
My dreams presage some joyful news at hand:
My bosom's lord sits lightly in his throne;
And all this day an unaccustom'd spirit
Lifts me above the ground with cheerful thoughts.
I dreamt my Julius came and found me dead –
Strange dream, that gives a dead man leave to think! –
And breathed such life with kisses in my lips,
That I revived, and was an emperor.
Well, Julius, I will lie with thee to-night.
Let's see for means:

(*Takes out the vial of poison*)

Come, cordial and not poison, go with me
To Julius's grave; for there must I use thee.

(*Enter* **NURSE**, *with a torch, mattock, &c.*)

Give me that mattock and the wrenching iron.
Hold, take this letter; see it is delivered
To-morrow morn to he that was my father.
Give me the light: upon thy life, I charge thee,
Whate'er thou hear'st or seest, stand all aloof,
And do not interrupt me in my course.

NURSE. I do beseech you, sir, come from this nest
Of death, contagion and unnatural sleep.

ROMEO. Why I descend into this bed of death,
Is partly to behold my darling's face;
But if thou, jealous, dost return to pry
In what I further shall intend to do,
By heaven, I will tear thee joint by joint
And strew this hungry churchyard with thy limbs:

The time and my intents are savage-wild,
More fierce and more inexorable far
Than empty tigers or the roaring sea.

NURSE. I will be gone, then, and not trouble you.

ROMEO. So shalt thou show me friendship. Take thou that:
Live, and be prosperous: and farewell, good nurse.

NURSE. (*Aside*) For all this same, I'll hide me hereabout:
His looks I fear, and his intents I doubt.

(*Retires*)

ROMEO. Thou detestable maw, thou womb of death,
Gorged with the dearest morsel of the earth,
Thus I enforce thy rotten jaws to open,
And, in despite, I'll cram thee with more food!

(**ROMEO** *opens the tomb.*)

(*Footsteps approaching, and whispers.*)

But soft! what voices? something doth approach.
What cursèd foot wanders this way to-night,
To cross my obsequies and true love's rite?
What with a torch! muffle me, night, awhile.

(*Retires*)

(*Enter* **BRUTUS** *and* **LUCIUS**, *bearing flowers and a torch.*)

BRUTUS. Give me thy torch, boy: hence, and stand aloof:
Yet put it out, for I would not be seen.
Give me those flowers. Do as I bid thee, go.

LUCIUS. (*Aside*) I am almost afraid to stand alone
Here in the churchyard; yet I will adventure.

(*Retires*)

BRUTUS. Sweet flower, with flowers thy final bed I strew:
O woe! thy canopy is dust and stones;
Which with sweet water nightly I will dew,
Or, wanting that, with tears distill'd by moans:
The obsequies that I for thee will keep

Nightly shall be to strew thy grave and weep.

ROMEO. This is that haughty traitor Marcus Brutus,
That butcher'd my dear love, and here is come
To do some villainous shame on his dead body:

(*Comes forward*)

Stop thy unhallow'd toil, vile murderer!
Can vengeance be pursued further than death?

BRUTUS. Good gentle youth, tempt not a desperate man;
Fly hence, and leave me: think upon these gone;
Let them affright thee. I beseech thee, youth,
Put not another sin upon my head,
By urging me to fury: O, be gone!

ROMEO. I do defy thy conjurations,
And apprehend thee; for sweet Caesar's soul
Is but a little way above our heads,
Staying for thine to keep him company:
Either thou, or I, or both, must go with him.

BRUTUS. This shall determine that.

(*They fight.*)

LUCIUS. O Lord, they fight! I will go call the watch.

(*Exit*)

(*They fight still;* **ROMEO** *stabs* **BRUTUS**.)

BRUTUS. O, I am slain!

(**BRUTUS** *takes* **ROMEO**'*s hand.*)

If thou be merciful,
Open the tomb, lay me with Julius.
Farewell, good Romeo.

(**BRUTUS** *abruptly pulls* **ROMEO** *toward him, running himself through on* **ROMEO**'*s sword.*)

Caesar, now be still:
I kill'd not thee with half so good a will.

(*Dies*)

ROMEO. This was the noblest Roman of them all:
    All the conspirators save only he
    Did that they did in envy of great Caesar;
    He only, in a general honest thought
    And common good to all, made one of them.
    Or am I mad, hearing him talk of Julius,
    To think it was so? O, give me thy hand,
    One writ with me in sour misfortune's book!
    I'll bury thee in a triumphant grave;
    A grave? O no! a lantern, slaughter'd soul,
    For here lies Julius, and his beauty makes
    This vault a feasting presence full of light.
    Death, lie thou there, by a dead man interr'd.

    (*Laying* **BRUTUS** *in the tomb*)

    How oft when men are at the point of death
    Have they been merry! which their keepers call
    A lightning before death: O, how may I
    Call this a lightning? O my love! my life!
    Why art thou yet so fair? shall I believe
    That unsubstantial death is amorous,
    And that the lean abhorrèd monster keeps
    Thee here in dark to be his paramour?
    For fear of that, I still will stay with thee;
    And never from this palace of dim night
    Depart again: here, here will I remain
    With worms that are thy chamber-maids; O, here
    Will I set up my everlasting rest,
    And shake the yoke of inauspicious stars
    From this world-wearied flesh. Eyes, look your last!
    Arms, take your last embrace! and, lips, O you
    The doors of breath, seal with a righteous kiss
    A dateless bargain to engrossing death!
    Come, bitter conduct, come, unsavoury guide!
    Thou desperate pilot, now at once run on
    The dashing rocks thy sea-sick weary bark!

Here's to my love!

(*Drinks*)

O true apothecary! Thy drugs are quick.
Thus with a kiss I die.

(*Dies*)

(*Enter, at the other side of the churchyard,* **CASSIUS**, *with a lantern, crow, and spade.*)

CASSIUS. The ghost of Caesar hath appear'd to me
Two several times by night; at Sardis once,
And, this last night, upon Philippi fields:
I know my hour is come. But, soft! Who's there?

(**NURSE** *comes forward.*)

NURSE. Here's one, a friend, and one that knows you well.

CASSIUS. Bliss be upon you! tell me, gentle nurse,
What torch is yond, that vainly lends his light
To grubs and eyeless skulls? as I discern,
It burneth in dead Caesar's monument.

NURSE. It doth so, noble sir; and there's my master.

CASSIUS. Romeo? my son?

NURSE. He bade me give you this.

(*Gives him the letter;* **CASSIUS** *reads.*)

CASSIUS. Alas, my wife—My wife is dead tonight.
Grief of my son's estrange hath stopped her breath.

(*He puts away the letter.*)

How long hath he been there?

NURSE. Full half an hour.

CASSIUS. Go with me to the vault. Fear comes upon me:
O, much I fear some ill unlucky thing.

NURSE. As I did wait under this yew-tree here,
I thought my master and another fought,
And that my master slew him.

CASSIUS. Alack, alack, what blood is this, which stains

The stony entrance of this sepulchre?
What mean these masterless and gory swords
To lie discolour'd by this place of peace?

(*Enters the tomb*)

Romeo! O, pale! Who else? what, Brutus too?
And steep'd in blood? Ah, what an unkind hour
Is guilty of this lamentable chance!
O me! this sight of death is as a bell,
That warns my old age to a sepulchre.
What's here? a cup, closed in my son's cold hand?
Poison, I see, hath been his timeless end:
O thou untaught! what manners is in this?
To press before thy father to a grave?
O, coward that I am, to live so long,
To see my best friends ta'en before my face!
See, what a scourge is laid upon my hate,
That heaven finds means to kill my joys with love.

(*Drinks the poison*)

O churl! drunk all, and left no friendly drop
To help me after?
(*to* **NURSE**) Come hither, woman:
In Parthia did I take thee prisoner;
And then I swore thee, saving of thy life,
That whatsoever I did bid thee do,
Thou shouldst attempt it. Come now, keep thine oath;
Now earn thy freedom: and with this good sword,
That ran through Caesar's bowels, search this bosom.
Stand not to answer: here, take thou the hilts;
And, when my face is cover'd, as 'tis now,
Guide thou the sword.

(**NURSE** *stabs him.*)

Caesar, thou art revenged,
Even with the sword that kill'd thee.

(*Dies*)

(*At last, the distant sound of fighting ceases and all is silent.*)

(*Enter some unsuspecting Commoners with candles and garlands of lavender intending to hold a vigil at Caesar's tomb. They will be the first to discover the bodies.*)

NURSE. (*as* **CHORUS**) There's nought so vile that on the earth doth live
But to the earth some special good doth give;
Nor aught so good but, strained from that fair use,
Revolts from true birth, stumbling on abuse.
Virtue itself turns vice, being misapplied,
And vice sometime's by action dignified.
A glooming peace this morning with it brings;
The sun, for sorrow, will not show his head:
Go hence, to have more talk of these sad things;
Some shall be pardon'd, and some punishèd:
For never was a story of more woe
Than this of Caesar and his Romeò.

(*Exeunt*)

SOURCES

The sources for this play are William Shakespeare's The Tragedie of Romeo and Juliet (1595) and The Tragedie of Julius Caesar (1599).

The author is indebted to the invaluable online resources of MIT's Shakespeare website (http://shakespeare.mit.edu/) and the Complete Moby™ Shakespeare.

NOTES ON THE TEXT

Every effort was made to preserve the rhythm, language and poetry of the original sources, particularly in the verse sections of the play.

Obviously, a certain amount of rewording is necessary as a practical matter of fusing the two texts. For example, combining the role of Juliet with Julius Caesar requires that numerous instances of "she" be replaced with "he," and "her" with "him", etc.

Whenever possible, replacement text is matched syllable-for-syllable. Thus, in verse sections, "lady" is replaced with "lordship," rather than "lord," to preserve the meter.

Always, the objective is to ensure that the original rhyme scheme, pronunciation and operative words are not inadvertently affected by modifications in the storyline.

ROMEO / ROMEÒ

The most significant aberration in the text involves the scansion of the title character's name, which, in Romeo and Juliet, is always treated as a two-syllable word, except when it comes at the end of a line of verse, in which case it is always three syllables.

In the present text, the character of Romeo has been melded with Mark Antony from Julius Caesar, which requires the replacement of "Antony" (3 syllables) in many lines of dialogue.

Rather than resort to a more obtrusive substitution—such as, replacing "Antony" with "Romeo, lad"—Romeo's name is simply employed interchangeably as a two- or three-syllable word, as needed to satisfy the verse, without regard to its placement in the line.

When "Romeò" occurs as tri-syllabic, it is indicated in the text with an accent over the third syllable.

DOUBLING OF ROLES

In Elizabethan and Jacobean England, it was illegal for women to appear upon the public stage. Hence, the plays of Shakespeare were written to be performed by an all-male company of actors with only a handful of female characters - largely secondary roles played by boys.

These male-heavy casts present a challenge in modern-day stagings, where the acting company is usually comprised of a more balanced troupe of men and women. To accommodate this, gender-blind casting[1] is recommended for the plays of Shakespeare, as well as gender-reversal[2], to adapt the plays to the available talent pool.

The following suggested breakdown for this play provides an abbreviated cast of 13 actors - eight men, five women:

MALE	FEMALE
Julius Caesar	Cinna
Marcus Brutus	Nurse
Caius Cassius	Portia
Romeo	Rosaline
Metellus Cimber	Benvolio / Cinna the Poet
Flavius Cimber / Conspirator	
Sampson / Lucius	
Gregory / Conspirator	

[1] Casting the best actor for the part, regardless of gender.
[2] Changing the sex of the character to fit the actor playing the part.

APPENDIX - THE WEDDING PRELUDE

In Romeo & Julius, the Conspirators oppose Caesar on the basis of his lifestyle, and the fear of measures he might enact on behalf of flamboyants like himself.

Theatre companies wishing to make the controversy of the play specific to the issue of gay marriage, can do so by inserting the following same-sex wedding scene. Caesar's personal stance on gay marriage can be made even more explicit, by letting him act as the Officiant in the scene.

This optional scene should be performed at the top of the play, as a prelude-before-the-curtain.

Romeo & Julius [Caesar]

Prelude:
The Wedding. Before a wedding chapel.

(*Enter* **OFFICIANT** *and* **SAME-SEX GROOM**)

OFFICIANT.
So smile the heavens upon this sacred act,
That after hours with sorrow chide us not!

GROOM.
Amen, amen! but come what sorrow can,
It cannot countervail the exchange of joy
That one short minute gives me in his/her sight:
Do thou but close our hands with holy words,
Then love-devouring death do what he dare;
It is enough I may but call him/her mine.

OFFICIANT.
These violent delights have violent ends
And in their triumph die, like fire and powder,
Which as they kiss consume: the sweetest honey
Is loathsome in his own deliciousness
And in the taste confounds the appetite:

Therefore love moderately; long love doth so;
Too swift arrives as tardy as too slow.
   (*Enter* **SAME-SEX BRIDE**)
Here comes thine angel: O, so light a foot
Will ne'er wear out the everlasting flint:
A lover may bestride the gossamer
That idles in the wanton summer air,
And yet not fall; so light is vanity.

BRIDE.

Good even to my ghostly confessor.

OFFICIANT.

Thy love shall thank thee, shortly, for us both.

BRIDE.

As much to him/her, else is his/her thanks too much.

GROOM.

Ah, sweetheart, if the measure of thy joy
Be heap'd like mine and that thy skill be more
To blazon it, then sweeten with thy breath
This neighbour air, and let rich music's tongue
Unfold the imagined happiness that both
Receive in either by this dear encounter.

BRIDE.

Conceit, more rich in matter than in words,
Brags of his substance, not of ornament:
They are but beggars that can count their worth;
But my true love is grown to such excess
I cannot sum up sum of half my wealth.

OFFICIANT.

Come, come with me, and we will make short work;
For, by your leaves, you shall not stay alone
Till holy church incorporate two in one.

                 (*Exeunt into the chapel*)

www.ingramcontent.com/pod-product-compliance
Lightning Source LLC
Chambersburg PA
CBHW072015290426
44109CB00018B/2244